Collins

need to know?

Party
Games

Sean Callery

Collins

First published in 2006 by Collins
an imprint of
HarperCollins Publishers
77–85 Fulham Palace Road
London W6 8JB

www.collins.co.uk

Collins is a registered trademark of HarperCollins
Publishers Ltd

09 08 07 06
4 3 2 1

© HarperCollins 2006

A catalogue record for this book is available from
the British Library

Produced by Lyra Publications
Managing editor: Emma Callery
Editor: Gillian Haslam
Designer: Bob Vickers
Photographer: Nikki English

For Collins
Series design: Mark Thomson

ISBN-13 978-0-00-721397-9
ISBN-10 0-00-721397-2

Colour reproduction by Colourscan, Singapore
Printed and bound by Printing Express, Hong Kong

Contents

Introduction

Games are fun. They give an opportunity for people of different characters and ages to mix, provide mental and social stimulation for all, and the lively games offer young ones a chance to let off some steam. Participants need to cooperate and communicate, encouraging them to get to know each other. However, above all, games are a fantastic way for families to get together and have a good time.

How this book works

This book describes more than 300 family games. You can dip into it when you need a few ideas for games for your own family, or if you're going to spend time with another family or if you are organizing a children's party. It also has ideas for larger gatherings of extended families and friends.

The games are divided into sections, but on page 182 you will also find listings of game by type, such as ice-breakers, those suitable for large groups or the very young, and outdoor games.

Text on each game includes the equipment and preparation needed and the lowest age for the game (e.g. 6+), plus clear playing instructions and ideas for variations.

Here's a simple checklist to help you choose and run the games:

Who's coming?
▶ How many will there be?
▶ Do they know each other? If not, name labels might be helpful, and plan in some ice-breaker games.

▶ Consider the age range of the people who will be there and choose some games that work well across the generations (older people may be more comfortable with acting and pencil and paper games than, say, relay races).

▶ Who will help run and supervise the games?

Where?

Make sure there's enough room for the games plus space for those who prefer to watch rather than participate.

If you are going to be outside, check safety and security and have a 'plan B' for bad weather.

Games are a great way to get people of different generations mixing and having fun together.

must know

Safe and sound
Safety must be a priority:
▶ Set clear rules for youngsters about where they are allowed to go.
▶ Be aware of choking hazards for young and old.
▶ Bare feet or shoes are safer to run in than socks.
▶ Wipe up spills and breakages immediately.

Introduction

must know

A planning checklist
Invitations
Choose the games
(see Order of play,
below)
Food or snacks and
drinks
Decoration
Clear the game-
playing space of
anything breakable
or dangerous, and
ensure any pets
are out of harm's
way.

When?

Some senior adults like to rest during the afternoon but are more perky in the evening, and others prefer the opposite. Children, in particular, can get very excited during games and it can be hard to calm them down after a series of lively activities. They may go to sleep better having calmed down following an afternoon of games rather than at the end of a hectic evening.

What else is happening?

▶ Are you feeding a large group?
▶ Are the games part of a larger celebration, like a wedding anniversary?

Order of play

Prepare a list of the games to be played and in what order. If players don't know each other, start with some ice-breaker games that encourage them to talk and get to know each other (see page 182). Alternate lively and quieter games to maintain interest and prevent things getting too hectic.

If food is being served, have a couple of calm, restful games afterwards to aid digestion.

Consider numbers, age ranges and how active most people will want to be.

Equipment

Some simple equipment, such as pencils and paper, balloons, etc., is required for some games. Check you have it and put it out ready.

Helpers

If it's a large gathering that you're planning, set up helpers specifically to:
▶ Supervise games to keep them safe and fair.
▶ Hand out and gather equipment.

▶ Keep an eye out for anyone who needs a little special attention, young or old.

Running a game

▶ Politely ensure that everyone who needs to follow instructions is listening. Give clear instructions and get one person to demonstrate any actions that are important to the game.

▶ Mix up the teams so that they are equal in both age and ability.

▶ Have a clear signal for the start and finish.

▶ Don't let one game go on too long.

▶ If appropriate, give winners' and consolation prizes plus awards for 'best sport', 'greatest effort' and so on.

▶ Be flexible and keep your sense of humour.

Players in running games should wear shoes or go barefoot: this is far safer than running in socks.

1 Acting games

There's a bit of a show-off in most of us, and acting games are the chance to let it out. They were particularly popular in the Victorian parlour as they offer a chance to socialize and perform among friends and family, young and old, without feeling as if you are 'on show'. Some love to shine in the limelight (quite often the people you least expect to!) while others shun it, but relish watching the fun – and the audience is vital to these games.

Acting games

There are tradititional and modern acting games in this section, together with a blend of calm miming games and frenetic performances. This selection also offers a chance for guests to play in teams or to take the stage as an individual. It's show time!

Blood potato

Ages: **10+** Numbers: **Any**

▶ A variation on 'wink murder' (see page 60).

Preparation: A darkened room or blindfolds.

This game is used as a warm-up by drama groups. Secretly appoint one person as your murderer. Dim the lights or don blindfolds and ask people to walk around the room. Whenever they bump into someone, they must say 'potato' apart from the murderer, who says 'blood'. On hearing this, the victim 'dies' dramatically with a terrified scream, removes their blindfold and moves out of the way to the edge of the room. The winner is the last 'potato' left.

Chain acting

Ages: **8+** Numbers: **Any, in equal teams**

▶ A mime-copying game.

Preparation: Some suggestions for mimes.

One team leaves the room while the other agrees something for them to act out. This can be anything from having a haircut to catching a train. They then call in the first player from the other team and tell them what they must act out. A second member is called in and the first player mimes the situation to them. The second player then has to act out what they saw to a third player, and so on until the last team member comes in and tries to guess what is being mimed. The teams then swap roles.

Variations: 1 An easier version is to ask them to pose as someone or something, such as Winston Churchill or a well-known pop star, or even the Statue of Liberty. **2** The mime has to link with your party theme, for example, walking the plank for a pirate party.

Charades

Ages: **7**+ Numbers: **5**+

▶ A famous traditional miming game.

Preparation: Some suggestions for what to mime if people are stuck for ideas.

One person shows with gestures whether they are acting a film, book or song. Then they indicate by raising fingers how many words are in the title and which word they will act, or whether they will act it as a whole. They can act part of the word by showing how many syllables it has (by tapping their arm with the relevant number of fingers) and

It's a film ...

It's on television ...

It's a book ...

It's a play ...

which one they are miming. The audience has to guess the title being acted out.

Variations: 1 Restrict the choices to just films, books or songs. **2** Widen the choices to allow any word at all.

Cops and robbers
Ages: **7+** Numbers: **8+**
▶ A quiet game using only the eyes.
Preparation: Pieces of paper with the words 'cop' or 'robber' written on them.

One person is sent out of the room – they are the tracker. Write either 'cop' or 'robber' on pieces of paper and give one slip to each player. There should be an equal number of cops and robbers, but they mustn't know which is which. Hide an object in the room and invite the tracker in. The robbers must sit still but steer the tracker towards the object with their eyes. The cops have to work out who the robbers are and accuse them. If they are right, that robber drops out of the game. If the copper is wrong, he drops out. The game ends when either the object is found, or all the robbers have been identified.

Dead ringer
Ages: **10+** Numbers: **Any**
▶ Can you do an impersonation of a celebrity?
Preparation: A list of famous people who are known to most of your guests.

Write the names of famous people on slips of paper, or number them on a list and ask the player to select a number. The player has to read an extract from a book or newspaper in the style of the celebrity. Everyone else has to guess who it is.

Diagnosis
Ages: **12+** Numbers: **Any**
▶ A game in which everyone plays their part.

Preparation: Some ideas for diseases (see below).

One brave volunteer is selected as the 'psychiatrist' and leaves the room. The other players agree an ailment, delusion or obsession that they must all display on his return. His job is to identify what everyone is suffering from. When the psychiatrist returns to the room, he asks individuals questions of any kind (apart from direct ones about the illness). All players must stay 'in character' as the game continues until the psychiatrist makes his diagnosis. He is allowed three attempts at this.

Some possible ailments are:

▶ Believing they are a famous celebrity.
▶ Agreeing with whatever is said.
▶ Answering the previous question.
▶ Obsessed with the weather.
▶ Believing they are in a movie.
▶ Thinking they are part of the circus.
▶ Aversion to words containing a certain letter (this is particularly tricky!).

Dumb crambo

Ages: **8+** Numbers: **Any, in teams**

▶ A traditional team miming game with a rhyming slant.

Preparation: A list of words that have many rhyming partners to suggest.

The first team chooses a word, and gives the other team a word that rhymes with it. So if their word is 'ball', they could say its rhyming partner is 'tall'. The second team's players have to mime a word that rhymes with the given word (so they could try 'call', 'fall', 'crawl' or 'haul'). The other team boos any wrong guesses, and claps when the correct word is acted out. If they cannot work out the word being mimed, the actor is allowed to say it. If you want to score this game, count how many guesses it took to identify the word.

did you know?

Dumb crambo
Dumb crambo was a very popular Victorian parlour game. These games are so called because they were usually played with guests, who would be entertained in the best room in the house: the parlour.

Laughter is very infectious, and the game of Frozen laugh is guaranteed to leave you chuckling.

Frozen laugh

Ages: **3**+ Numbers: **6**+

▶ A lively game best played in a circle.

Preparation: Light object (such as a balloon or handkerchief) to throw.

Throw the object in the air. The players have to laugh constantly until it lands, when they have to freeze into silence. Anyone who makes a noise is out, until there is only one player left, or until it is clearly time to move on!

Variations: 1 Throw a feather or a toy on a parachute. **2** Stop and start silly music as the cue.

In the manner of the word

Ages: **8**+ Numbers: **Any**

▶ A fun miming game.

Preparation: None.

Adverbs are words that tell you how something is done, like 'carefully', 'nervously' or 'slowly'. Send one player out of the room, and the group must agree an adverb. When the player returns, he can ask anyone in the room to do something in the manner of the word, for example take off their shoes, welcome him to the party or close the door. Then he guesses what the adverb could be. Up to four mimes and guesses are allowed for each word. Some ideas for adverbs: artistically, angrily, anxiously, shyly, slyly, slowly.

Variation: A pair leaves the room and returns, acting in the style of the adverb. The rest of the players guess the word.

Invisible animal

Ages: **8**+ Numbers: **6-10**

▶ Can you work out what you are passing on?

Preparation: None.

All sit or stand in a circle and the first player secretly imagines an animal and silently pretends to pass it to the next person. It is most fun if this is done quite slowly so there are many opportunities to handle the creature. The receiver must handle it the same way, and pass it on. When it reaches the last player he has to guess what the animal is.

Variations: **1** Young children might benefit from being allowed to look inside a bag for ideas of what to pass on – soft animals are a good choice, but remind them they must pretend it is real. **2** Allow passing of objects rather than animals. This is trickier. **3** Mime activities such as riding a bike or eating candy floss.

King elephant

Ages: **8**+ Numbers: **Any**

▶ A movement and memory game.

Preparation: None.

Everyone sits in a circle and chooses an animal they can act with their hands (for example, flexing your arm and hand with fingers closed suggests a snake). All the animals and gestures must be different. Someone is chosen to be King Elephant and a space must be created between them and the person to one side, who becomes the end of the line. Everyone demonstrates their action in turn to the other players. Now the King Elephant does his action and that of any other player in the circle. That player must perform his own action and that of any other player, who takes the next turn, and so play continues. If someone makes a mistake, they go to the end of the line and everyone shuffles along one space. The aim of the game is to become King Elephant, which happens when the King makes a mistake and goes to the end of the line: everyone moves up one place and there is a new King Elephant. The old King now takes on his replacement's animal action (which is where people really start to get confused!). This game should be played as fast as possible.

Living mirror

Ages: **4**+ Numbers: **6**+

▶ This is less of a game and more of a drama activity, although you could award prizes for the best pair.

Preparation: None.

In pairs, players agree who will be the 'mirror' and who is the 'reflection'. The latter must copy every movement made by their partner. Feet must stay still at all times. Call out a series of actions, such as brushing your hair, tying a shoelace or eating spaghetti. Swap roles regularly.

Variation: Put on music for the 'mirrors' to move to.

My name is ...

Ages: **10**+ Numbers: **Any**

▶ A 'celebrity' miming and questioning game.

Preparation: A list of suitable celebrities most people will know.

A player leaves the room while the others think of a celebrity they should know. When they come in, the player can ask five questions about the person, to which the others can only answer 'Yes' or 'No'. After that, they have to do an impression of who they think the celebrity is.

Variations: 1 If the game is too easy, reduce the number of questions that can be asked. **2** Extend the range of 'celebrities' to include famous people in history or family members.

One more

Ages: **8**+ Numbers: **Any**

▶ A miming game requiring excellent memory.

Preparation: None.

Players sit in a circle. One player makes a movement, such as clicking his fingers or sticking out his tongue. The next player must repeat this and add an action of their own. Play continues with anyone who forgets a movement retiring from the game until you have a winner.

Orchestra!
Ages: **6**+ Numbers: **Any**
▶ A musical miming game.
Preparation: None.

One player is made conductor. He decides which instruments each player must pretend to play, then starts to clap. All players must pretend to play their instruments as realistically as possible, complete with musical sounds. The conductor can stop clapping at any time and point to an individual, which is their signal to perform a solo. Any other player who continues playing during this solo is out. Play until the 'orchestra' tires, swapping roles regularly.
Variation: Each player, including the conductor, chooses an instrument to silently pretend to be playing, starting when the conductor begins. However, at any time the conductor can switch to someone else's instrument, at which point everyone has to copy him, while the person being imitated must put their hands over their ears. Then the conductor switches back to their instrument. Anyone failing to change movements is out.

Pose the word
Ages: **8**+ Numbers: **Any**
▶ An adjective-miming game.
Preparation: Pieces of paper, each with an adjective written on them.

Adjectives are describing words, such as 'sad', 'happy', 'surprised', 'embarrassed'. Write lots onto different pieces of paper and put them in a pot. Each player takes one and has to strike a pose that depicts it. The rest of the group guesses the word.

Shadow play
Ages: **5**+ Numbers: **Any, individually or in teams**
▶ Can your hands act?
Preparation: A projector or powerful light and a screen or white sheet, plus slips with names or pictures of animals.

Children find it impossible to resist making hand shapes on a projector screen, so they'll love this game. Each player takes a slip and has to make shadow shapes with their hands to represent their animal for the others to guess. Play individually or in teams.

What's my job?

Ages: **8+** Numbers: **Any**

▶ An old favourite where you guess occupations.

Preparation: List of jobs to suggest.

Show a player one of the occupations on your list. They must mime it to the rest of the group, who must guess the job. Some suggested jobs include: pop star, brain surgeon, refuse collector, auctioneer, magician, model, TV chef, dog trainer.

Variation: Allow questions, to be answered only 'Yes' or 'No'.

What's that in English?

Ages: **8+** Numbers: **Any, individually or in teams**

▶ A chance to play at being a funny foreigner.

Preparation: Phrasebooks in foreign languages.

Each team or player has a book giving common phrases in a foreign language. If you don't have enough books, you could prepare some phrases on paper in advance. The team or player has to act out and say the phrase, while the other players guess its meaning and wording. Score points for acting quality and accurate answers.

Where are we going?

Ages: **10+** Numbers: **Teams**

▶ A team miming, spelling and guessing game.

Preparation: None.

One team leaves the room and agrees a place they could be going, such as Manchester. They come back in and one person at a time mimes an action to match one of the letters, in the order they appear in the word. For example the first player could mime 'Marching', the second 'Arguing', the third 'Nibbling' and so on. When all the mimes are finished, the other team has 5 minutes to decide what the destination was, so it makes sense for them to note down their ideas while the actions are going on. They can ask for repeats of some of the mimes. If they guess it correctly, they take a turn. If not, the acting team has another go, with a different destination.

Variations: 1 All destinations have to be countries. **2** The chosen words could be on other themes, such as foods.

Who's in charge?

Ages: **6+** Numbers: **6+**

▶ A lively movement game with several variations.

Preparation: None.

One player goes out of the room. He will be the guesser. The others agree on a leader, whose movements and actions they start to copy. When the guesser returns he has to pick out who is leading the group.

Variations: 1 The actions must all be silent. **2** The actions are rhythms, which can be created using any part of the body.

Zoo game

Ages: **3+** Numbers: **Any**

▶ A simple and quiet animal miming game.

Preparation: None.

Ask for a volunteer and whisper the name of an animal in their ear. They have to mime that creature silently and the players guess what it is.

Animals can be small and bouncy ...

... or long and elegant.

2 Action games

These are games where the players have to carry out an action. Only a few involve tough physical activity (you'll find more arduous games in the 'High-energy' and 'Racing' sections). You are more likely to be asked to throw accurately, or to hide something (even a person, in the Coat game), or just swap places. Therefore many of these games are suitable for all generations.

Action games

A wide variety of actions and movements are used in these games. Some involve just two players at a time, watched by an audience eager to find the best strategy for when it is their turn. Others will keep everybody on their toes at all times!

Balloon catch
Ages: **6**+ Numbers: **6**+
▶ A balloon catching game best played in a circle or with the players in a line.
Preparation: Some inflated balloons.
   Give everybody a number to remember. Drop a balloon and as you drop it say one of the numbers. That player tries to catch the balloon before it lands.
Variation: Say two numbers so that two players compete to catch the balloon.

Beat the gallows
Ages: **7**+ Numbers: **4-10**
▶ How fast are your fingers?
Preparation: A length of string tied with a loose knot to form a noose.
   Sit the players in a tight circle, each with one forefinger touching in the middle of the group. The hangman places the noose over the set of fingers and walks around the circle. On the shout of 'Death!' he pulls on the string to tighten the noose around the digits. Anyone who fails to remove their finger is 'dead' and out of the game.

Beat the guard

Ages: **8+** Numbers: **Any**

▶ Steal the object without being heard.

Preparation: A chair, blindfold and a book.

Blindfold one player and sit them on a chair with a book underneath it. He is the guard. Everyone else sits in a circle and the leader indicates who must take a turn at trying to remove the book, but every time the guard hears a sound he points to where it came from. He is not allowed simply to sweep his arms around. If he is pointing at the thief, they are out. Anyone who succeeds takes the place of the guard. Allow the guard three guesses before changing roles.

Variations: 1 Substitute keys for the book – much trickier! **2** Too easy? Lay sheets of newspaper, plastic or bubble wrap around the chair. **3** Still too easy? The thief must walk round the circle with their treasure before sitting down. **4** If playing outdoors, the guard can be equipped with a water pistol or a squeezy bottle to fire at the thief.

Blind blow

Ages: **Any** Numbers: **Any**

▶ An activity for individuals that is also particularly good fun to watch.

Preparation: A table, a table tennis ball and a blindfold.

The object of this game is to blow the table tennis ball off the table. This may sound easy, but the player is blindfolded, taken three steps from the table, turned round three times, then returned, so they will find it tricky to even find the table, let alone the ball!

did you know?

Blind blow
This game is a modern variation on a Victorian 'household amusement', which involved ladies and gentlemen blowing a ball of wool across a table.

Soft fabrics are best for blindfolds. You can always fold them over a few times if they are thin enough to see through.

Blind man's buff

Ages: **6**+ Numbers: **8**+

▶ A traditional identity-guessing game.

Preparation: Blindfold.

You need an obstacle-free area to play this. Blindfold one player and put them in the middle of the circle. Everyone in the circle keeps moving round in one direction until the 'blind man' claps three times, points at someone and guesses their name. If they are correct, they swap places. If not, a player comes into the circle and the 'blind man' has to catch them and guess their identity by feeling their face, hair and clothes.

Variations: 1 Players circulate singing a song. The 'blind man' claps, points at someone and tells them to do a forfeit, like 'Cry like a baby' or 'Say the alphabet', after which they try to guess the performer's identity. **2** Cut straight to the chase and have the 'blind man' patrolling a (safe) area until he catches someone and has to guess their identity. **3** 'Blind man' stands in the centre of a seated circle while the players change seats, then he sits

did you know?

Blind man's bluff

▶ A Victorian version of this game was called 'Blind man's wand', in which the 'blind man' would hold a stick, which would be grabbed by another child, who would then be asked three questions. The better they disguised their voice as they answered, the less likely they were to be identified. Sometimes they had to imitate animals instead.

▶ This game has a history of at least 2,000 years - there are references to it being played in Greece at about the time of the Roman Conquest. In Spain it is called 'Gallina Ciega', which means blind hen, while in France it is named 'Colin Maillard', after a French lord who continued to fight a battle after he had been blinded.

on any player's lap. No words are spoken, but that person must whistle a tune and the blind man guesses the performer.

Blow it

Ages: **3+** Numbers: **Any**

▶ A game that needs lots of puff.

Preparation: Paper shapes, cut to a party theme, such as animals.

In advance, prepare some paper shapes about the size of a postcard. Put one in front of each player, and their challenge is to send it as far as they can with three blows.

Bucket goal

Ages: **4+** Numbers: **Any**

▶ A simple throwing game.

Preparation: Buckets and plenty of balls.

Set out a row of buckets. There could be one for each child or team, or you could use coloured buckets and have a scoring system, with each bucket worth a different number of points. Players have to stand behind a line and throw balls into the buckets. Make it fair by having them line up and go to the back of the queue after each throw, successful or not. The softer types of low-bouncing balls are better because they won't rebound out of the bucket, or place some crumpled fabric in the base of the bucket. If the containers tip over easily, weigh them down with a brick, or half-fill them with water if playing outside (otherwise set them on a plastic sheet).

Variations: 1 Use beanbags instead of balls. **2** Adjust the throwing distance according to the team's ability.

Button button

Ages: **Any** Numbers: **Any**

▶ An old parlour game.

Preparation: A button or similar object.

Appoint a 'tailor' who will do the guessing later. Everybody else stands in a line or circle, hands cupped slightly open. One person is

given the button, and they move along the line,
pretending to (or did they really?) drop the button
into one set of hands. Then everybody calls to the
tailor 'Button, button, who has the button?' and he
has to guess who is holding it.

Variation: Everybody takes it in turns to move along
the line, so that the button could be passed on
several times.

Change places

Ages: **6+** Numbers: **8+**
▶ A swapping game.
Preparation: None.

Players sit in a circle with one person in the
middle. The leader calls out who has to change
places, choosing statements such as, 'Change if
you are barefooted' or 'Change if you are wearing
trousers'. Everyone who matches the description
must change their seat, and meanwhile the leader
tries to sit in an empty place, leaving someone
stranded in the middle, who then becomes the new
leader, and so the game starts all over again.

The coat game

Ages: **4+** Numbers: **10 (or preferably more)**
▶ A surprisingly tricky observation and memory
game.
Preparation: Large coat, or sheet.

One person leaves the room. The rest change
their positions, and a sheet or coat is placed over
someone. When the guesser returns, they must try
to identify who is under the sheet. It is much harder
than it sounds!

Crocodile alert

Ages: 5+ Numbers: **Any, in pairs**

▶ A good game for sleepovers.

Preparation: One sleeping bag needed per pair.

Zip each pair into one sleeping bag. The leader then shouts 'There's a crocodile coming!' and the pairs race to escape out of the bag. Last pair out gets eaten up.

Discs and domes

Ages: **Any** Numbers: **Any, in equal teams**

▶ A lively game best played outdoors or in a large space.

Preparation: A large set of stackable plastic cones, which are available from play equipment shops.

Divide the players up into the 'disc' team and the 'dome' team, showing them how a disc one way up makes a dome shape, and the other way up makes a bowl-like disc. Hand one team all the cones, which they then lay out on the ground in 'their' shape. After 30 seconds, let the other team loose to turn over as many as they can – while the first team are allowed to turn them back. No physical contact is allowed and only one person can touch a cone at any time. After a couple of minutes call 'time' and count up the scores.

Don't sink the boat!

Ages: **Any** Numbers: **Any**

▶ A tense water-pouring game, best played outside.

Preparation: A die, a shallow bowl of water, a teaspoon and some jam-jar lids.

Float the lids like boats in the bowl. Players take it in turns to throw the die. Whoever throws a six must pour a teaspoon of water into one of the lids. If the lid sinks they are out. Winner is the last child still in the game.

It takes a little practice to get the technique right for the egg cup race.

Egg cup race

Ages: **8+** Numbers: **Two equal teams**

▶ A game that requires a lot of puff.

Preparation: Each team needs two egg cups and a table tennis ball.

The first players put the table tennis ball in one cup and place the other near it. The aim of the game is to blow the table tennis ball through the air from one egg cup to the other. As soon as a player achieves this, his teammate takes over to repeat the act. The first team to finish wins.

Egg throw

Ages: **6+** Numbers: **Any, in pairs**

▶ A throwing game where you get messy if you mess up.

Preparation: An egg for each pair.

Play this game outdoors. Each pair stands facing each other and throws the egg between them. After every two successful catches they both take a step back. Play continues with longer and longer throws until the egg gives up!

Variation: Try using balloons half-filled with water.

Fishing

Ages: **5+** Numbers: **2-6**

▶ You should have seen the one that got away!

Preparation: A large bowl holding a fair number of paper clips (about ten per player), plus a wire coat hanger for each player.

Fill the bowl with water and pour in the paper clips. Players bend their coat hangers to create a hook (or you can do this for them in advance). Then they try to hook out paper clips, the winner being whoever ends up sitting proudly by the biggest pile of office supplies.

French cricket

Ages: 5+ Numbers: 4+

▶ A simple racket and ball game for any number of players.

Preparation: A ball and tennis racket or bat. This is definitely an outdoor game.

Give one child a tennis racket. They are the batsman. They must stand with their feet together and are not allowed to move their feet at all. The rest of the players are bowlers and fielders. They throw the ball, aiming at any part of the batsman's foot or leg below the knee. If the ball touches these areas, or if the batter moves his feet, the batter is out. If the batter hits the ball he can be caught 'out', otherwise whoever fields the ball must bowl from where they picked it up.

Variations: 1 If fielders catch the ball after one bounce, the batsman is out. **2** Allow younger players to move their feet to turn to face the bowler.

French cricket works well with just about any number of players.

Fruit basket

Ages: **5+** Numbers: **16+**

▶ A 'fruity' variation on musical chairs, requiring a fairly large space such as a hall.

Preparation: A chair for each player.

Players sit in a circle (the 'fruit basket') and you allocate each to a 'fruit', so that there are about four people in each group of fruits. Then you call out one of the fruits, and all those people must stand up and change seats, except that you remove one chair, leaving one 'fruit' stranded and out of the game. If you say 'Upset the fruit basket' everyone has to switch seats.

General post

Ages: **8+** Numbers: **Any**

▶ An old seat-swapping game.

Preparation: Chairs for everyone and a blindfold.

All but two people sit on chairs in a circle. Each says the name of a town or destination, which is written down by the postmaster (the host). The other non-sitting person is the postman, who stands, blindfolded in the middle of the circle. The postmaster then calls out two of the places on his list. The two people who said those locations must immediately swap places. If the blindfolded postman intercepts someone, or sits in a vacated chair, he is replaced by the person who didn't make it to their destination. The game really comes to life when the postmaster chooses to call 'General post!', which means everybody must change seats.

Good morning, madam

Ages: **8+** Numbers: **Any**

▶ A riotous variation of 'Snap'.

Preparation: A pack of cards, jokers removed.

Deal out all the cards, using two packs if there are more than seven players. Everyone then holds their cards face down so that they can't see them, and on their turn, places one card face up on the pile in the middle. The object of the game is to get all the cards. When an ace appears, everyone slams their hand down on top of it, the first hand (the one that is now on the bottom) winning the pile. When a king is seen, everyone stands up and salutes. If the card is a queen, everyone shouts 'Good morning, madam'. If it is a jack, the players stand up and curtsy. In each case, the first person to complete the relevant action gets the cards.

The pace should be kept fast, and it can be useful to appoint a referee as disputes (good-natured, of course) are likely.

did you know?

Parties in Victorian times
Prosperous Victorians saw children's parties as a way to display their wealth and, at the same time, to ensure their children understood social etiquette, such as taking turns and knowing how to give instructions.

Grandmother's footsteps
Ages: 5+ Numbers: **Any**
▶ A traditional and calm game of movement that needs lots of space.
Preparation: None.

One person goes to the end of the space and stands or sits with their back to the others, who line up at the other end. They have to creep up and tap the person (grandmother) on the shoulder, but she can turn round at any time and say the names of anyone she saw moving. They must return to the start point.
Variation: Put two or three coats out and divide the children into that number of teams. Whoever touches the 'grandmother' must be wearing the coat. If they work as a team, they can hide each other as someone puts the coat on.

Guard the gate is a pretty hectic target game where everyone is part of the action.

Guard the gate

Ages: **5+** Numbers: **6+**

▶ Roll the ball through the gap.

Preparation: A suitable ball – large for young children, or a tennis ball for older players.

Everyone sits in a circle with a gap between them and their neighbours. Each gap is a 'gate' and the aim of the game is to roll the ball through one of them. If this happens, the two players either side of it drop out, players move around the circle to make the vacated gap smaller, and play continues until only one or two players remain.

Handful

Ages: **5+** Numbers: **Any**

▶ An estimating game.

Preparation: A bowl of small wrapped sweets.

Players sit in a circle around the bowl of sweets. Invite a volunteer to pick up a handful of them, but they must then close their hand up and guess how many they have got. If they guess the correct number or a number less than the total, they keep the number they said. If their estimate is more than the number in their hand, they have to put them all back. Use wrapped sweets to keep this game hygienic.

Hit and catch

Ages: 7+ Numbers: **6+**

▶ A baseball practice game.

Preparation: A baseball or cricket bat and a tennis ball.

The batsman throws the ball up and hits it, then places the bat on the ground at a right angle to where the ball was collected. If a fielder catches the ball, they become the batsman. If not, they roll the ball as hard as possible towards the bat. When the ball hits the bat, it should flip up in the air and the batsman has to catch it, otherwise the fielder takes his place. If the ball just bounces back along the ground, the batsman gets another hit. Change places every five hits.

Hoopla

Ages: 3+ Numbers: **Any**

▶ A hoop-throwing game.

Preparation: Rubber rings, or cut small hoops from thick pieces of card, targets.

Players try to throw their hoop (or hoops) to land over a target. This could be a water-filled bottle, or a prize such as a packet of sweets.

Hot potato

Ages: 3+ Numbers: **6+**

▶ A passing game for young children.

Preparation: An object to pass round.

Children pass any object round the circle. It can be a ball, beanbag or even a potato. They have to imagine it is hot and so must pass it on quickly. When an adult helper calls 'Hot!', whoever is holding the 'potato' is out and play continues.

Variations: 1 Use music to signal when to start and stop. **2** Play outdoors with a water-filled balloon (swimwear or change of clothing required!).

watch out!

Dropped ice cubes will melt a little, which could cause players to slip, so have a cloth handy to wipe the floor.

Ice and pick race

Ages: **6+** Numbers: **Equal teams**

▶ A slippery passing race.

Preparation: Ice cubes and two bowls per team, plus a stock of toothpicks.

Give each team a bowl of ice cubes, and put the other bowls at the end of your 'track'. The aim of the game is to get all the ice cubes to the second bowl, using toothpicks. After each player has delivered their ice cube, they tag the next member of their team. Dropped ice cubes have to be picked up with the toothpicks.

In the bucket

Ages: **5+** Numbers: **Any**

▶ Hit the buckets in the right order.

Preparation: Five buckets and five small balls.

Put the buckets in a straight line, going away from the players. The aim of the game is to throw one ball into each bucket, starting with the nearest and ending with the furthest. Each turn ends if the ball misses or enters the wrong bucket, and you can score a point for each accurate throw. Putting water or fabric in the buckets will stop them tipping and prevent the balls bouncing out.

Ingredients

Ages: 4+ Numbers: **Any**

▶ A quiet sorting game.

Preparation: A small bowl with a mixture of dried beans, lentils, rice and raisins. A blindfold and timer.

The blindfolded player has to sort the mixture into groups of the same ingredient. Do a test run to check it can be done in less than, say, 2 minutes. Time each attempt to find the winner.

Jet journey

Ages: 4+ Numbers: **Any, in pairs**

▶ How far will the plane go?

Preparation: A good supply of paper planes.

Players can, of course, spend a happy time making the planes for the game first. Then the first player throws a plane and stands still. The second player picks up the plane where it landed, and throws it back. Players cannot interrupt the flight of the plane, and must pick it up where it lands and try to send it further back the other way. It will be clear from where they end up standing after, say, 5 minutes who sent it on the longest journey.

Jigsaw race

Ages: 4+ Numbers: **Any**

▶ A jigsaw with a difference.

Preparation: A bag with a Christmas card, picture, photograph, map or diagram for each player or team, cut up into an equal number of pieces.

Ingredients is a calm and gentle game. You could use buttons and differently shaped beads instead of dried foods.

Each player or team races to piece together the jigsaw. You can make the task harder or easier according to how many pieces you cut the image into – label each bag with the number of pieces.

Key chain

Ages: **6+** Numbers: **Equal teams**

▶ A classic team game.

Preparation: A length of string and key for each team.

The string is threaded up and down inside the outer clothes of the whole team. When you say 'Go!' the team must pass a key along the string to reach the last player.

Variation: Store the keys in the freezer before the game.

Key hunt

Ages: **6+** Numbers: **Any**

▶ A concealment game requiring teamwork.

Preparation: A key, or another object to conceal, such as a marble, coin or sweet.

One player (who will be the hunter) sits in the middle of a circle formed by the other players. The hunter closes her eyes and counts to ten while the players pass an object between each other. Players continue to do this when she opens her eyes, with everyone either passing the object or pretending to. She has another ten seconds or so to name who has the key. If she is right, they swap places, and if not the game is repeated. Allow three guesses.

Kick bowling

Ages: **4+** Numbers: **Any**

▶ A mix of soccer and bowling skills.

Preparation: Skittles and a ball.

Set up five skittles (or large plastic bottles half-filled with water) in a 'V' formation. Players have to kick a ball from a set distance and see how many skittles they knock over. This can be played individually or in teams. Adjust according to ability by having different types of ball (e.g. soccer ball, tennis ball).

The 'longest' game

Ages: **Any** Numbers: **Even teams**

▶ A team game where you're not quite sure what you're letting yourself in for.

Preparation: Some ideas of different challenges.

The leader asks for a volunteer from each team, saying they are looking for the longest, widest, shortest, most or some other superlative. When all the volunteers are ready, the leader sets the challenge, which could be to find who has the longest tongue or can hold their breath the longest, or has the widest smile. Teams can score points for each round.

Just how wide is that smile?

Some ideas for challenges are:

▶ Longest: hum, hair.
▶ Widest: spread of feet.
▶ Biggest: smile, feet, ears.
▶ Most: buttons, pockets, pennies.

Matches

Ages: **6+** Numbers: **Any**

▶ A deceptively simple activity game.

Preparation: A box of matches, cocktail sticks or some other small objects.

Place about 50 matches on the table. Each player is allowed to take up to six at each turn. The aim of the game is to avoid having to pick up the last match.

Mega bubble

Ages: **5+** Numbers: **Any**

▶ A bubble-making challenge.

Preparation: Tub of water mixed with $1/3$ cup liquid detergent and 2 teaspoons of glycerin; wire hangers or pipe cleaners.

You may want to experiment with your bubble-making mixture first (some people add sugar to help the bubbles form). Each team moulds their hanger or pipe cleaner into a loop and the challenge is to find who can make the biggest or longest-lasting soap bubble.

Memory

Ages: **6+** Numbers: **4–8**

▶ An old game that tests observation and memory.

Preparation: Pack of playing cards or specially prepared pack (see variation).

Place the cards face down in a regular grid formation. Explain that each card has a partner of the same colour and number, so that, say the two of clubs is paired with the 2 of spades, while aces of diamonds and hearts are partners. Each player takes it in turns to turn over two cards. If they match, he keeps them and turns over another two. If the turned-over cards are not a pair, they are returned. The aim of the game is to collect as many pairs as you possibly can.

Variations: 1 For younger children, use a smaller pack (make sure it has pairs in it). **2** For an easier version, only turn one card back over each time. **3** Make your own cards using matching or similar images cut from magazines, or from family photographs.

Mingle mingle

Ages: **8+** Numbers: **10+**

▶ A good 'warm-up' game for large groups.

Preparation: None.

The leader calls out a number between three and ten. Everybody has to get into groups of that number, chanting 'Mingle mingle', and all in the group must be touching in some way. Anybody left over is out, but can return for the next round unless you continue until you have one winning group.

Variation: Get people to gather together in groups of, say, the same birth month, or colour of hair, eyes or front door.

Minty pass

Ages: **6+** Numbers: **Even teams**

▶ A mint-passing race using straws.

Preparation: Packet of mints or other sweets with holes in and a plastic straw for each player.

This is a team game where the mint is threaded onto a straw. The sweet must be passed through the team, always on the straw, which can only be held by the teeth. So the first player passes the mint onto the straw of the second player, and so on. If the sweet is dropped, the team must start again from the beginning.

Variation: Cocktail sticks could be used instead of straws, but beware of injuries as they are sharp.

Mouth to mouth

Ages: 6+ Numbers: Equal teams

▶ A passing game using spoons.

Preparation: One spoon per player, plus objects to pass along.

Games that require concentration and coordination can be just as much fun to watch.

The aim of this game is to pass an object along the team using spoons held in the mouth. The objects can be anything fairly light and unbreakable, such as ping pong balls, tennis balls, grapes or raisins. If the object falls to the floor, the team must start again, and it must never be touched by hand (players might need to hold the spoon by hand to pick up objects).

Variation: Make the contest a 'best of five games'.

Mummies

Ages: **Any** Numbers: **Any**

▶ A very silly dressing game.

Preparation: Plenty of rolls of toilet paper.

This game can be played by pairs or small groups. The aim is to wrap one person up in toilet paper so that they look like an Egyptian mummy. Set a time limit of between 3 and 5 minutes, and the best 'mummy look-alike' wins.

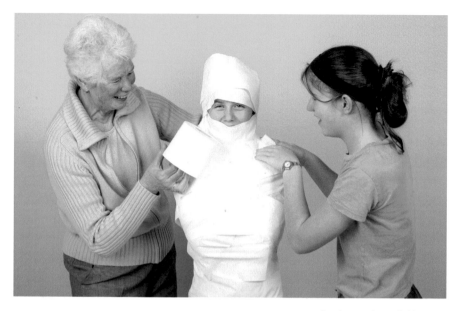

Murder in the dark

Ages: **8+** Numbers: **6 or (preferably) more**

▶ A long-established and much-loved detective game.

Preparation: Slips of paper and a hat (optional).

Put a cross on one slip of paper and a circle on another. The rest stay blank. Players take one slip each: the cross selects the murderer (who keeps quiet about it) while the circle appoints the detective (who can don the hat and leaves the room for the next part of the game). The lights are switched off, and everybody should move slowly round the darkened room until the murderer whispers 'You're dead' in his target's ear, and moves away. The dramatic scream of the victim will prompt the turning on of lights, and everybody stays where they are. The detective returns and asks questions to try to identify the murderer – who is the only person allowed to lie, unless directly accused of being the perpetrator. The detective has two guesses (three with a group of more than ten) of who did the deed.

Stock up on loo rolls if you are going to play Mummies, and don't forget to unravel your models.

Newsprint catwalk

Ages: **Any** Numbers: **Any**

▶ A dressing-up game using newspaper.

Preparation: Plenty of newspaper, pins and sticky tape.

This game is best played by groups, whose job is to dress one member in newspaper sheets (making holes is allowed, either by tearing or supervised use of scissors). Set a time limit of between 5 and 10 minutes, then have a catwalk competition for the most adventurous fashions.

Noughts and crosses

Ages: 7+ Numbers: 11+

▶ A 'human' version of this popular game.

Preparation: Nine chairs in three rows of three.

Divide players into teams by gender, by the colours they are wearing, or just by asking one side to form their arms into a cross. Play the game using the chair grid, with captains telling players where to sit.

Variation: Ask each team a quiz-type question in turn. If they get it right, they can place a player. Play then moves to the other team.

Object bingo

Ages: 8+ Numbers: **Any**

▶ A variation on the number-collecting game.

Preparation: Ask everybody to bring nine small objects (which can include watches and rings). Prepare cards with nine squares marked out in a grid.

Everybody places their nine objects in the squares on their card. The first person selects an object and holds it up, calling out what it is. That and any similar objects anyone else has on their card are removed, and play continues with the next caller. The winner is the first with an empty card.

Odd or even?

Ages: 7+ Numbers: **Any**

▶ A good ice-breaking game.

Preparation: Ten cocktail sticks, paper clips or wrapped sweets for each player.

Players walk around the room and as they meet someone, they put a few cocktail sticks or sweets in their fist, hold it out and ask 'Odd or even?'. The second player guesses and they then check if the fist held an odd or even number of sticks. If their guess was right, the player is given one stick. They then swap roles and repeat the game. The winner is the one with the most sticks after 10 minutes.

One knee

Ages: 7+ Numbers: **Any**

▶ A throwing and catching game.

Preparation: A soft ball.

Players stand in a circle and throw the ball to anyone else in the group. If someone drops the ball they have to put one knee on the ground. If they catch it the next time, they stand up, but if not, they go down on both knees. Play continues with players recovering from or incurring further penalties in this order:

▶ One knee
▶ Two knees
▶ One arm
▶ No arms (you catch the ball on your lap)
▶ One eye
▶ Out.

The winner is the player who stays in the game the longest.

Open the parcel

Ages: 7+ Numbers: **Any**

▶ A circle game that keeps everyone involved.

Preparation: Wrap a gift in several layers of paper. You also need oven mitts or a pair of other gloves, a hat and scarf, and two dice.

Players sit in a circle and take it in turns to roll the two dice (get them to throw them in a biscuit tin to keep them within reach). If someone scores 5, they have to put on the hat, scarf and gloves before starting to open the package. In the meantime, players continue to roll the die and a fresh score of 5 means that player takes over the task.

Party blowers

Ages: 4+ Numbers: **Any**

▶ A perfect party race.

Preparation: Party blower and empty matchbox for each player.

The excitement of Party blowers is heightened by the noises the blowers make as they are used to push the missile.

The aim of this game is to get the matchbox (or similarly light but stable object) from one end of the course to the other, moving it only by puffing into the party blower. Keep an eye out for anyone who is trying to push the object with their inflated blower.

Penny drop

Ages: 3+ Numbers: **Any**

▶ An old favourite at summer fetes.

Preparation: A bucket of water, 50p piece or £1 coin, and a supply of 2p pieces.

Put the most valuable coin in the bucket. Players must stand and drop 2p pieces from head height into the water. If the coin ends up on top of the original coin, they win it.

Piggy in the middle

Ages: **6+** Numbers: **3+**

▶ An ancient throwing and catching game that keeps all participants on their toes.

Preparation: A soft ball.

Everyone stands in a circle (or if there are only three players, two stand opposite each other) apart from the 'piggy', who is in the middle. Players throw the ball to each other past the piggy. If she catches it, she swaps places with the last thrower.

Variation: If the piggy so much as touches the ball, she swaps with the thrower.

Pyramids

Ages: **6+** Numbers: **Any, in teams**

▶ A practical activity good for small groups.

Preparation: A deck of cards, cocktail sticks or pieces of card for each team.

This is a straight and creative challenge: who can make the tallest pyramid simply using the materials that are provided?

Quasimodo

Ages: **5+** Numbers: **Any**

▶ A listening and tagging game.

Preparation: A bell and blindfolds for each player.

All but one player is blindfolded. Their task is to try to catch the sighted player, who must move around the space while ringing the bell.

Rattle

Ages: **5+** Numbers: **Any**

▶ Where did it go?

Preparation: Blindfold, lidded plastic or paper cup with some dried beans or small stones, or a baby's rattle.

All players sit in a circle around one blindfolded player. The rattling container must be thrown between the players, who must count to five in their heads before passing it on. The blindfolded player must point to the person they think is holding the rattle. If they are right, they swap places.

Red letter

Ages: **6+** Numbers: **Any**

▶ A traditional playground game, requiring a large space.

Preparation: None.

One person goes to the far end of the space to be the letter picker, and informs the group what the 'red letter' is to be for the round. Other players stand in a line some distance away. The letter picker calls out any letter, and each player who has that letter in their name takes a step forward. If the 'red letter' is called, no one must move. If they do, they must go back to the start. The winner is the first player to reach the letter picker.

Variations: 1 Take one step for each time the letter appears in your name. **2** Hop or jump instead of stepping.

Ring on the string

Ages: **3+** Numbers: **6+**

▶ A classic game of concealing and guessing.

Preparation: A long piece of string or fishing line, and a ring or bead.

48 | need to know? Party Games

Thread the ring or bead onto the string or fishing line and tie it to make a large circle, which everybody sits around, holding hands. One player leaves the room and when he re-enters he stands outside the circle while players pass the ring along the string secretly. When the leader calls 'stop', the player guesses who has the ring.

Rockets

Ages: **4**+ Numbers: **4**+

▶ A simple balloon-launching game that can be played in teams.

Preparation: Uninflated balloon for each player, plus a target.

Set up or agree a target, which could be a picture or object related to your party theme. Give everybody an uninflated balloon and ask them to blow it up without tying the knot (some young players may need help with the inflating). On an agreed signal, everybody lets off their balloon and watches it zoom away. You can, if you wish, award marks for who gets nearest the target (with a bonus for hitting it), or for the furthest distance that has been travelled.

Variation: Play in teams, with each team having balloons of the same colour.

Roll for treasure

Ages: **3**+ Numbers: **6–10**

▶ A dice-rolling thriller.

Preparation: A small-sized prize, cocktail sticks and a die.

Put all the cocktail sticks around the prize, which can be wrapped up. Players take it in turns to roll the

Turning round with a balloon between you sounds so simple, and is so very tricky!

---

watch out!

Balloon safety
Children choke more easily than adults, and balloons do represent a choking risk.
► Avoid using balloons at all with children under four years old.
► Store balloons – whether inflated or not – away from children.
► Pick up bits of burst balloon straight away.
► Polyester balloons (sold under the trade name Mylar) are safer than latex.
► Dispose of old balloons safely.

---

die, removing the number of cocktail sticks they scored with the die. When all the sticks have been removed, players count how many they have and whoever has most wins the prize.

Roundabout
Ages: **6+** Numbers: **Any number of pairs**
► A slow-moving race with balloons.
Preparation: One blown-up balloon per pair, plus some spares.

Each pair stands facing each other with the balloon resting between their stomachs. The task is to complete five full turns on the spot without dropping the balloon.
Variation: Pairs could race in the same position.

Sardines
Ages: **5+** Numbers: **Any**
► A classic variation of Hide and seek.
Preparation: None.

One person hides while the others wait. Then the hunt is on to find that person and silently join them in whatever space they chose. Eventually everybody will be crammed together in one place.

Scavenger hunt
Ages: **6+** Numbers: **Any**
► An individual or team hunting game.
Preparation: Hide or locate at least ten

things and list them on sheets of paper, (optional) bag to hold them for each team or player.

Each team or individual is given the list of hidden items. These could include specific toys, dice, photographs, sweets or paper clips. They write or draw the location of the objects, or (if you put out enough of each) put one sample in their bag. First to complete the set wins.

Variations: 1 Instead of objects, provide categories such as 'something yellow', 'something you put in your mouth' or 'a square inside a circle' (such as a framed mirror with those shapes). **2** Older children could be sent on a hunt in the street, seeking certain road signs, berries or door colours. Set clear boundaries of how far they should go and about staying together, or have an adult with each group. **3** Play word or picture hunt using old magazines, equipping each team with paper, scissors and glue in order to stick down the required image or letters.

The Shirt swap game takes a bit of working out, which makes it very satisfying.

Shirt swap

Ages: **6+** Numbers: **Any, in equal teams**

▶ A dressing-up race that calls for teamwork.

Preparation: One over-sized shirt for each team.

Dress one player in each team in a large shirt (do up any buttons except the collar). Then they must join one hand with that of another team member. The task for the whole team is to transfer the shirt to the next person without the pair releasing their hands. They'll eventually work out (you hope!) that this can be done by removing the sleeve from the outside arm and lifting the shirt over the head, then sliding the garment across inside out for the partner to put on by the reverse method.

Shovelboard

Ages: 6+ Numbers: **Any, individually or in teams**
▶ An indoor, homemade version of an ancient target game.
Preparation: A table top, chalk or masking tape, rulers and coins.

Shovelboard is an ancient game with many indoor and outdoor variants. It works well as a team game. On the table top, use chalk or masking tape to mark out the 'board' as follows:
▶ For the sides, mark lines about 15cm (6in) inside the longest edges of the table.
▶ At one end of the table and at right angles to those already made, mark two more lines. The top one should be about 15cm (6in) from the end and the second 15cm (6in) below that.

Now it's time to play. Players score by pushing coins (or 'pucks') with rulers from the bottom end of the table, hoping to reach the scoring sections:
▶ The large area in the middle of the table is a no-score area.
▶ The area above the first line is a low-scoring area.
▶ The area above the second line (furthest away from the players) is a high-scoring area.
▶ Coins that fall off or go over the outside marker lines do not score.

Teams take it in turns to push one coin at a time (so there may be an opposition coin in place when a team takes a turn). It is acceptable to aim your coin to move others, from your team or not. When both teams have finished using all their coins, the board is scored as follows:
▶ Coins partly off the top of the table in the high-score area score 3.

▶ A coin completely in the high-score area scores 2.

▶ A coin in the low-score area or on the line between it and the high-score area scores 1.

You could play towards an agreed total of points, or score by winning rounds, or set a time limit and calculate the total score.

Splash

Ages: **5+** Numbers: **Any**

▶ A water-carrying game, with variations, best played outdoors.

Preparation: Chalk or cardboard or hoops to be used as the 'stones'.

Mark two lines of five circles with chalk or use cardboard or hoops to make five stepping stones just too far apart to step easily. Players have to move along the stepping stones carrying a full plastic cup of water. The winner is whoever has the most water left.

Variations: 1 Players have to wear flippers. **2** They also have to carry a book on their head, or roll a ball as well. **3** People get on all fours and have a plastic bowl of water placed on their back. **4** If your players are good at this, try it as a relay.

Spoons

Ages: **8+** Numbers: **6–12**

▶ A card-collecting game with kitchen utensils!

Splash is a great game to play outdoors on a sunny day.

Preparation: A pack of playing cards, jokers removed, and one spoon for each player.

Players sit on the floor or around a table. They must all be able to reach the pile of spoons, of which there should be one less than the number of players. Four cards each are dealt, the remainder are put in a pile in the middle. The aim of the game is to collect four of a kind, such as four kings. The dealer takes a card from the pile on the table and passes a card (it can be the same one) to the player on his left. That player then chooses which card to pass on, and so on, but the dealer continues to pick cards from the pile on the table so the game flows pretty fast. As soon as someone has four of a kind, they pick up one of the spoons. Everybody else now does the same, and the one player left without a spoon is now out. Another spoon is removed and play continues until there are two players fighting it out for the last piece of cutlery.

Variation: For a shorter game, adjust the pack so that there are only enough cards for four cards per player. So six players will need 24 cards, from nines to aces. Players simply pass one card to their left with each turn.

Squeeze

Ages: **6+** Numbers: **Any**

▶ Can you spot the squeeze?

Preparation: None.

Players stand holding hands in a circle, with one 'spotter' in the middle. One person squeezes the hand of their neighbour, who must then pass on the squeeze. If your left hand is squeezed, you squeeze to the right, and vice versa, but you can change the direction of the squeeze at any time. If the spotter correctly identifies someone who has just squeezed, they swap places.

Squeeze murder

Ages: **10+** Numbers: **10+**

▶ A squeezy version of wink murder (see page 60).

Preparation: Blank cards, one marked with a cross.

Everyone is given a slip of folded paper. The one marked with a cross appoints the murderer. Everyone now sits in a circle, holding hands. The murderer squeezes the hand of someone to their right or left anything from one to ten times. That person must pass on one less squeeze, and so on until someone receives only one squeeze, which is their signal to die – as dramatically as they like. Anyone can accuse another player of being the murderer, but if they are wrong, they are out of the game.

Variations: 1 The leader chooses the murder by tapping them on the head when everyone is sitting with their eyes closed. Anyone can accuse their suspect and the leader will tell them if they are right, or are now dead. **2** Someone who wants to accuse the murderer must say 'I suspect (name)', but that person cannot respond unless another player says 'I second it'. If they are right, the game ends, but if they are wrong, they both die.

Swaps

Ages: **5+** Numbers: **Any, in two equal, even-numbered teams**

▶ Who swapped what with whom?

Preparation: None.

Allow the teams to study each other for one minute, then send one team out of the room. Everyone in the remaining team must swap one item of clothing with a team member. Invite the other team back and they must say who swapped what with whom. It may be worth making a note of who did swap what, as young children can be very vague about such matters!

Swingers

Ages: **5+** Numbers: **Any**

▶ A strange-looking race

Preparation: Two pairs of old tights, plus a cucumber or banana, orange or potato.

This game is named after the motion required. Put a cucumber, banana or an orange down one leg of the tights, and then tie them round the player's waist so that the weighted leg hangs down. Their challenge is to use the tights to move a potato or orange (or a boiled egg) from one side of the room to the other. They cannot use their hands at all. You could run this as a race or as a timed challenge.

Treat stealer

Ages: **6+** Numbers: **6+**

▶ The more you remember, the more sweets you get.

Preparation: Two packs of cards and a supply of individually wrapped sweets and chocolate bars, or other small identifiable treats (three per player).

Everyone sits in a circle with the treats in the middle. Each player is dealt three cards, which they place face up in front of them. The leader now turns over one card at a time from the second pack. If any of these cards match one a player has in front of him, he takes a treat from the middle and hides it somewhere in his clothes. Tell everyone to watch carefully who gets which treat, and when everyone has three, gather in the cards, shuffle them and deal one card to each player. Only they must know what it is. Now return to turning over a card at a time from the (also shuffled) second pack. When a player spots a match, he shows his card and states which treat he wants and who has it. If he is right, he keeps it, but if he is wrong he gives that person one of his treats. Keep playing until everyone has had a chance or two. Then eat the sweets!

Up Jenkins!

Ages: **8+** Numbers: **Two even teams of about 5 per team**

▶ An old and well-loved parlour game.

Preparation: A coin.

The teams sit opposite each other at a table. One team is given a coin, which the players must pass to each other under the table until the leader of the other

Up Jenkins! has been creating laughter and confusion at parties for many years.

did you know?

Up Jenkins!
A Victorian version of this game originating in Hertfordshire was known as Tippit. The hidden object was a small nut or a marble.

team says 'Up Jenkins!' At this point they must raise their clenched fists above the table. When the opposing leader says 'Down Jenkins!' they must crash their fists down on the table. The leader can then say 'Creepy crawly', which means the players must wriggle their fingers, or 'Flat on the table', when palms must be flattened, or 'Wibbly wobbly', which means fists must be turned up and down again. At any stage the leader can guess who has the coin, and if he is right, it transfers to his team. If not, play starts again.

Variation: Players have to guess who has the coin, and which hand it is in.

Water bowling

Ages: **5+** Numbers: **Any**

▶ A simple, outdoor water-throwing game.

Preparation: A start line, with a bucket of water 5m (15ft) away, and some skittles (plastic bottles with a little water for stability will do) about 3m (10ft) further on.

Players take it in turns to run to the bucket, fill a plastic cup from the bucket and throw the water to knock the skittles over.

Variations: 1 Adjust the throwing distance according to the abilities of the players. **2** Use coloured bottles and have a scoring system

What's the time, Mr Wolf?

Ages: **5+** Numbers: **Any**

▶ A traditional chasing game for young children.

Preparation: None.

One person is Mr Wolf, who stands at one end of the space. The others call out 'What's the time,

Mr Wolf?' and he says a time between one and 12 o'clock. The children have to take that number of steps forwards. However, when the wolf replies 'Dinner time!' he chases them and whoever he catches is the new wolf.

Where's the candle?
Ages: **10+** Numbers: **Any, in teams**
▶ A direction-giving game.
Preparation: A candle for each team, so different colours will help.

A row of lit candles is placed on a table, one per team. Teams stand at the other end of the room, and one player in each is blindfolded. Their task is to blow out their team's candle. Other players are allowed to give them directions, using only the words 'left', 'right', 'up', 'down' and 'blow'.

watch out!

Candle safety
When playing Where's the candle? keep someone by the table at all times to ensure safety, and make sure all long hair is tied back.

Whistleblower
Ages: **4+** Numbers: **Any**
▶ A hectic ball-passing game.
Preparation: Ball, plus a whistle and blindfold.

All stand in a circle around one player who is blindfolded and given the whistle. Players pass the ball round the circle until the blindfolded player blows his whistle, when whoever is holding the ball is out. Play continues until you have a winner.

Who swapped?
Ages: **4+** Numbers: **8+**
▶ A quiet memory game.
Preparation: Blindfold needed.

Blindfold one person and sit them in the centre of the circle. Give all the others a piece of paper with a number or letter on it. Call out two numbers or letters, and those two people must swap places, passing the player in the centre. Then she removes her blindfold and guesses who swapped.

Variation: Instead of two people swapping, send one out of the room and the blindfolded person has to spot who is missing.

Wink murder

Ages: **Any** Numbers: **8+**

▶ A classic and popular game.

Preparation: Slips of paper, one marked with a cross to appoint the murderer.

Draw the folded papers to select a murderer, who kills by winking at his victims, who in turn should die as loudly and theatrically as possible. A useful rule is that they must wait 30 seconds before doing this, which helps add interest to the game if players are walking around the room. Anyone can accuse another of being the murderer, but is out of the game if wrong. The murderer wins when only two other players are left.

---

must know

You're out

Many of these games involve players being 'out'. Some younger players can get upset and feel rejected when this happens. Be ready with a hug and praise for anyone who is 'out', and have little treats like sweets, biscuits or toys ready to dispense. These children can also help judge the next round if appropriate, or you could have a special area where they can draw or hear a story. If being 'out' for the rest of the game is too much to bear, they could be 'out' for 1 minute and then return.

Variations: 1 Players can only challenge the murderer by naming him to a victim before they die. **2** The murderer kills by sticking out their tongue (very popular with children who can't wink properly). **3** A very effective variation is Handshake murder where everybody has to circulate and shake hands, but the murderer has a previously agreed signal, such as gently tapping the victim's palm.

Wool tangle

Ages: **Any** Numbers: **Any, in teams of four if possible**

▶ An old game requiring quick fingers.

Preparation: Each team needs a chair and a ball of yarn.

Each team has one minute to tangle their wool around a chair. Then the teams move to another chair and the race is on to untangle the wool and wind it back into a ball. No deliberate breaking of the wool is allowed, and the chair cannot be moved.

You can imagine the Wool tangle game originating with a harrassed mother telling her brood to sort out the mess they had made when her back was turned!

3 Food games

Although some of these games are fairly decorous, most are an excuse to get really messy or to eat as much or as fast as you can. So they are likely to appeal to the child in all of us. Do be prepared for the sticky residues some of these games create, both in the room and on the players. It is also important to check for any food allergy or intolerance among the, no doubt willing, participants.

Food games

Food has been used in party games for centuries, from apple bobbing to eating apples or doughnuts suspended just out of reach. It is probably worth saving these games for the end of the party to avoid too many spoiled appetites.

Apple bobbing

Ages: **Any** Numbers: **Any**

▶ A traditional party game that can get people rather wet.

Preparation: Bowl of water, apples.

This is a simple challenge: with your hands behind your back, can you get the apple out of the water using your mouth? Play this outside or lay down plastic sheeting first. It is worth following this game with Marshmallow bob (see page 69).

Take a breath and dive in ...

... then re-surface triumphant (if soggy)!

Apple on a string

Ages: **Any** Numbers: **Any**

▶ A traditional party game, especially at Halloween.

Preparation: Cored apples and string.

Tie the string in a loop through the core of the apple, then hang several at a height people can reach (you could make them kneel down). The race is to finish eating your apple first, without touching it with your hands.

Chocolate detective

Ages: **Any** Numbers: **Any**

▶ A quiz that players will really enjoy whether they are right or wrong!

Preparation: A selection of chocolate bars.

Cut the bars up, and put one piece of each on numbered plates (use labels or write on the underside with a marker pen), noting which bar went where. Now microwave the portion until it starts to melt and squash it down with a spoon. When the chocolate has cooled, invite players to eat it and identify which bar it came from. Have plenty of water on hand – this is a thirsty game.

Variation: Just remove the wrapping from chocolate bars and re-wrap them in foil. Players have to guess the product by tasting them.

Crisp challenge

Ages: **Any** Numbers: **Any**

▶ Can you identify the flavour?

Preparation: A selection of crisps in different flavours.

Put different flavours of crisps in numbered bowls, noting down which one is where. The challenge is for players, or teams, to identify the flavours. You could be really sneaky and include the same flavour twice to see if the players can spot it.

---

watch out!

Microwaves
Microwaves do not heat chocolate evenly, so use a low setting, take your time and let the food cool well before you let people try it – otherwise it could burn tender young mouths.

Eat the choc

Ages: **4+** Numbers: **6+**

▶ A very lively chocolate-eating game.

Preparation: Chocolate slab bar, plate, blunt knife and fork, hat, gloves and scarf. A die.

In the middle of a circle formed by the players, place the chocolate on the plate, next to the cutlery and clothing. Players roll the die and if they get a six they have to put on all the clothes and try to eat the chocolate with the knife and fork. While they are doing this, the others continue to roll the die and anyone throwing a six takes their place.

Variations: 1 For large groups, use two dice and double the clothes. **2** Use chocolate buttons with younger children. **3** Use oven mitts instead of the other clothing.

Few things grab a child's attention more than the prospect of some chocolate.

Feast

Ages: **4+** Numbers: **Equal teams**

▶ A team eating game.

Preparation: Bag or bowl of foods for each team.

Prepare sets of the same foods for each team. The winner will be the first team to consume the lot. Every member of the team must eat at least one item, and the fun is in watching the negotiations about who will eat what from a selection that could include a tin of sardines, pickles, a slice of onion, a clove of garlic, unsweetened cold black coffee, chocolate, a cracker, etc.

Find the doughnut

Ages: **Any** Numbers: **Any**

▶ An eating contest with a difference.

Preparation: Blindfolds and doughnuts.

Ring doughnuts are perfect for this, otherwise push a skewer through the doughnut and feed string through. Tie the doughnut from a beam (or from the branch of a tree if you can play outside). The doughnut should be at head height. Blindfold the player and turn them on the spot three times. Now they have 15 seconds to find and start to eat the doughnut without using their hands.

Fluffy bunnies

Ages: **Any** Numbers: **Any**

▶ An excuse to talk with your mouth full!

Preparation: Marshmallows.

Players sit or stand in a row and are each given a marshmallow to put in their mouth. They must say the phrase 'Fluffy bunnies'. Now a second marshmallow goes in and they must say the phrase again, and so the game continues until a player is unable to speak or is spotted chewing the sweet, when he is out of the game, until you have a (rather fat-cheeked) winner. Bibs or bins are handy for this game.

Variation: For a healthier version, use slices of banana, and players have to say the phrase 'Chubby monkeys'.

Jelly face

Ages: **6+** Numbers: **Pairs**

▶ A jelly-blowing game.

Preparation: Fairly runny jelly and a short tube (like a sweetie tube).

Put jelly into the tube, and have one person hold it while two players put their faces near each end. On the shout of 'Jelly face', each player blows into the tube until one of them gets a face full of jelly. It's useful to have towels or damp face cloths handy after this game!

Lace race

Ages: **Any** Numbers: **Any**

▶ How fast can you consume the liquorice?

Preparation: A supply of strawberry or liquorice laces.

Each player has one lace. The race is to eat it as quickly as possible without using hands – the game is fun to watch people making the most extraordinary faces as they hoover up the sweet.

Licky licky

Ages: **6+** Numbers: **Any**

▶ An impossible challenge that is fun to watch.

Preparation: Plenty of doughnuts.

This is not so much a game as a challenge: can you eat a doughnut without licking your lips? It sounds easy, but it isn't!

It is quite hard to chew when you are laughing.

Marshmallow bob

Ages: **Any** Numbers: **Any**

▶ A messy game well worth playing after apple bobbing (see page 64).

Preparation: Bowl of flour, marshmallows.

With their hands firmly behind their backs, players have to hunt down the marshmallow in its floury home using their mouths.

Variation: Find the cherry that lurks in a bowl of whipped cream.

Off your head

Ages: **Any** Numbers: **Any, in pairs or in equal teams**
▶ A no-hands feeding race.
Preparation: Selection of dry, flat foods such as biscuits, crackers or crisps.

The eating player sits on a chair, leaning back, and their partner places a biscuit or cracker on their forehead. The race is to get it into your mouth and eat it without using your hands.
Variation: Turn it into a team game by having players line up behind the chair and take their turn when the player before them has finished their food.

Popcorn missiles

Ages: **Any** Numbers: **Any**
▶ A popcorn-throwing contest with a 'catch'.
Preparation: Chair, popcorn.

If possible, play this game outside or on a washable floor. This game could be played by individuals or in teams, in which case each team starts with a bowl of popcorn. One person per bowl sits on a chair a short distance away, say, 2m (6ft). The challenge is to throw the popcorn into their mouths. The team that makes the least mess on the floor wins.

Spaghetti dice

Ages: **Any** Numbers: **Any**

▶ A die-rolling contest that can get really frustrating.

Preparation: Ten strands of spaghetti per player, plus one dice and a bowl.

Each player has ten sticks of dry spaghetti. They take it in turns to throw the die, placing the matching number of strands of spaghetti in the bowl. Soon most players will have one or two sticks left, but if they throw over that figure they have to take that many strands back out of the bowl. First to get rid of all their spaghetti wins.

Spaghetti relay

Ages: **6+** Numbers: **Equal teams**

▶ A fiddly relay.

Preparation: A bottle and pair of gloves for each team, plus a supply of dry spaghetti.

Set bottles up a few paces from the starting line, where the teams are waiting with their spaghetti sticks. Each player must put on gloves and run up with one strand of spaghetti to feed into the bottle, returning to give the gloves to the next team member. Broken strands don't count and must be replaced. First team to place, say, ten strands is the winner.

Sweet scavenge

Ages: **Any** Numbers: **Any**

▶ A very messy sweet-seeking game.

Preparation: Bowls filled with baked beans, mushy peas, custard, or cornflakes (which will be far less mucky, but a lot less fun).

This is a messy game, so play it outside or protect your floor with plastic sheets. Put a sweet in the bottom of each bowl. The contestants might like to put on

Children will do anything to get a sweet!

aprons (or remove shirts) before they dunk their heads in the bowls, seeking the sweet with their mouths (no hands). First to succeed wins ... a bag of sweets (or a can of baked beans).

Takeaway rice

Ages: **6+** Numbers: **2-6**

▶ A fiddly task requiring patience and dexterity.

Preparation: Bowl of rice grains, a glove and bottle for each player.

Players must pick up grains of rice, one at a time, from a bowl and drop them in a bottle. However they must be wearing gloves (thick ones such as gardening or oven gloves are particularly cruel).

The tasting game

Ages: **6+** Numbers: **Any**

▶ A game for food detectives.

Preparation: A set of bowls, each with different foods, blindfolds.

Number or label each bowl and note down which food is in which bowl. Players try a spoonful of each one blindfolded, saying what they think each food is – the leader should write their comments. Have some water to hand to help them clear their tastebuds. The winner is whoever correctly identifies the most foods.

Suggested foods include: ketchup, chutney, pickle, baked beans, tinned tomatoes, fresh herbs, crisps, noodles, chocolate, yogurt, but you could also slip in a squeeze of toothpaste to confuse the palettes.

Variations: 1 Mix two foods into one container and get the players to taste them together and identify the ingredients. **2** Use liquids only, such as cola, diet cola, cold tea and coffee, water, lemon juice, soda water, soup, fruit juices. **3** Just use powders in very small quantities such as salt, pepper, sugar, flour, mustard, gravy granules, coffee, drinking chocolate, bicarbonate of soda. Players can taste these by dipping a wet finger into the powder.

You're crackers!

Ages: **8+** Numbers: **Any**

▶ An impossible challenge that is fun to watch.

Preparation: A packet of unsalted cheese crackers and a glass of water.

Challenge players to eat three crackers without taking a sip from the glass of water. The challenge is hard because the crackers soak up the moisture in the mouth, making it impossible to swallow the food.

4 High-energy games

Variety keeps our interest alive, and a few really energetic games will bring an extra glow to many of your guests. Very active games offer a chance for the young to let off steam and release pent-up energy. Although these games don't all call for Olympic level sprinting, they do require active participation and, often, a fair degree of flexibility or a lot of puff. So a gentle warm-up, maybe in the form of a few rounds of of Simon says (see page 175) might be advisable. Less active guests may like to play the role of cheerleader for these games.

High-energy games

Many of these games are ideally played outdoors, or in a large and safe indoor space. It is worth scheduling them before any food is served as they don't aid digestion, and your more lively guests will actually want to sit still for a while after playing them.

Ankle race

Ages: **5**+ Numbers: **Any**

▶ A surprisingly tricky race!

Preparation: An agreed racing course.

Set a course to race, and the only condition is that players must hold their ankles throughout the course. This one is great fun to watch and is best played outdoors on grass.

Balloon bash

Ages: **4**+ Numbers: **Any**

▶ A game that is fun to watch as well as to play.

Preparation: Inflated balloons, rolled up newspaper and a blindfold.

Everyone stands in a circle apart from one blindfolded player in the middle, who is equipped with a rolled-up newspaper. A balloon is released into the circle and the blindfolded person is allowed three attempts to hit it. Score three points for a first-time strike, two for the second attempt and three if they hit at the third go. Bursting the balloon scores five extra points.

Balloon hockey

Ages: **6**+ Numbers: **Even**

▶ A highly competitive balloon-hitting game.

Preparation: A supply of long and round balloons, plus a goal such as a cardboard box.

Each player has a round balloon in a different colour, plus a long balloon, which will be the bat or stick. Set up a goal – it can be an open box on its side. The aim is to 'score' by hitting the round balloon into the goal. You'll need to referee this one!

Bang!

Ages: 5+ Numbers: **Any**

▶ A balloon-popping game for two players.

Preparation: A supply of balloons and string.

Tie a balloon to the left leg of each player. The aim is to burst your opponent's balloon with your free leg.

Variations: 1 Try playing with more players. They could play individually or as a team (with balloons of the same colour).

2 Hold the balloons against the stomach.

It can be surprisingly difficult to burst someone's balloon, especially when you are trying to protect your own.

Blindfold shootout

Ages: 4+ Numbers: **Any**
▶ A balloon-kicking game with a twist.
Preparation: Inflated balloons or beachballs, a blindfold and a goal.

Set up the goal (it can just be a cardboard box open at the side) and stand a player a short distance from it with the balloon at their feet. Tie on the blindfold and turn them round three times. Now they have to kick the balloon and try to score a goal. This game is fun to watch!

Bowl race

Ages: **6+** Numbers: **Equal teams**
▶ A relay race with a difference.
Preparation: Bowl with objects for each team.

Put the players into equal teams and have a bowl containing an equal number of buttons or beads (or objects that match a party theme) for each team. Set the bowl at one end of the running area, and put all the teams at the other end with an empty bowl for each. One child from each team runs and collects a button, putting it in the empty bowl. This is the signal for the next child to go, until the first bowl is empty.
Variations: 1 Use sweets instead of buttons. **2** Add a handicap like having to hop, or run backwards.

Broom game

Ages: **6+** Numbers: **Any**
▶ A dizzy activity that is very funny to watch.
Preparation: Clear a large area and fetch a long-handled broom.

Ask someone to stand in the middle of an open space and give them a broom. They must hold the upright brush high and turn round ten times, looking up at the bristles. Then ask them to walk to you across the space. They will find this very difficult! Grass is the best surface as people tend to fall over.

Bubble wrap promenade

Ages: **Any** Numbers: **Any**

▶ A quiet and gentle game.

Preparation: Long length of bubble wrap.

Few people can resist the simple pleasure of bursting the bubbles in bubble wrap packaging material, but resist you must in this game. Appoint a referee to judge, and invite contestants to walk along the stretch of bubble wrap as quietly as possible, without bursting the little air-filled sacks.

Variation: Turn it into a deportment challenge by having the walker balance a book on their head.

Cat and mouse

Ages: **5+** Numbers: **8+**

▶ A game of 'Tag' played in a circle.

Preparation: None.

All players stand with hands joined in a circle, apart from one 'mouse' inside it and one 'cat' outside it. The mouse must keep moving, creeping out under the linked arms and running round the ring while the cat tries to catch him or her. The mouse is allowed back inside the ring but only for a few moments. The cat is not allowed inside the circle but can reach through to tag the mouse. When the mouse is caught, they become the cat and a new mouse is chosen.

Caterpillars

Ages: **5+** Numbers: **Even teams**

▶ A race for those with young knees.

Preparation: None.

Each team stands in line. The front person kneels and the next player kneels and grabs the ankles of the player in front. This continues until each team forms a 'caterpillar'. Now it is a straight race to reach the finishing line but the caterpillar must stay intact. If it breaks, the team must re-start.

Chain race

Ages: **5+** Numbers: **Two equal teams**

▶ The whole team ends up running together in this outdoor race.

Preparation: Two cones or chairs.

Set the cones or chairs about 20m (60ft) apart. Divide the players into equal teams and put one group behind each cone. The first person in each team runs a circuit round the opposite cone and returns to their team. No one is allowed to obstruct them. For the second circuit, they must run holding hands with their next

High-energy games are exciting and a chance to let off some steam.

teammate. This is repeated until by the final round the whole team is running, all holding hands.

Variation: Run a 'centipede' race where each person has to hold onto the waist of the person in front, making a giant conga line. If the line is broken, the team has to go back to the start.

Clothes peg challenge

Ages: **6+** Numbers: **Pairs**

▶ A game of nip and tuck.

Preparation: Two clothes pegs for each player.

Players face each other, each equipped with two clothes pegs. The aim of the game is to attach both your clothes pegs to your opponent's clothes. Each time you achieve this you score a point, then play continues or a new challenger enters the fray.

Corner to corner

Ages: **5+** Numbers: **Four equal teams**

▶ A featherweight contest.

Preparation: Four feathers and four tables.

Clear the room of furniture apart from a small table in each corner. Teams stand in the corners and the aim of the game is to get their feather to land on the table in the opposite corner. Feathers can only be blown, and if they land short of the target, must be picked up and blown from there. A referee is useful in this game but don't ask them to stand in the middle of the room!

Variation: Play across the floor, this time blowing ping pong balls into a box.

Crab race

Ages: **6+** Numbers: **Any**

▶ A rather uncomfortable race.

Preparation: None.

You need a forgiving surface such as carpet or grass for this race. Individuals have to race in the crab position, achieved by

> **watch out!**
>
> **Feather allergies**
> Some people react badly and quickly to the presence of feathers. Check with your guests if this is likely to be the case. You could always use artificial feathers instead of real ones.

lying on your back then raising yourself up on your arms and legs. They then agree whether to move sideways, backwards or forwards. You can run this race with individuals or as a relay.

Cup race

Ages: **Any** Numbers: **Any, in teams**

▶ A very silly race.

Preparation: Each team will need a piece of string about 4m (12ft) long, plus a paper or light plastic cup with a hole in the centre.

Each team threads the cup onto the string, which is then stretched taut with a player at each end. All the cups should be at the same end, rims at the edge. The aim of the race is to blow your cup to the other end of the string. Check no teams lower one end of the string to help the cup along.

Dodge the ball

Ages: **7+** Numbers: **Any**

▶ An old throwing and running game to be played outdoors or in a large space.

Preparation: Soft ball.

One child has a soft ball. They throw it, aiming to hit other children on or below the knee. Anyone hit joins them and they work as a team, passing the ball to each other as well as aiming at the others, until everyone has been hit.

Variation: No moving when you hold the ball.

Down the alley

Ages: **6+** Numbers: **Any even number between 10 and 20**

▶ A goal-scoring game using a balloon.

Preparation: An inflated balloon (plus some spares).

Sit the players in two equal-length lines facing each other about 1m (3ft) apart. The space down the middle is the 'alley'. Number each player, starting at one. The even numbers are now one team, mixed in with the opposing odd numbers (it is worth checking people understand this before you go any further). Now agree the even and odd goals, which are the opposite ends of the alley. The aim of the game is to pat the balloon into the opposition goal. Players must remain seated, and cannot hold or throw the balloon.

Variation: The two opposite lines form a team each and the scoring method is to hit the balloon over the other team's heads so that it lands on the floor. Players can lean back but cannot change position.

Dragon's tail

Ages: **Any** Numbers: **Any**

▶ A very old variation of 'catch'.

Preparation: None.

You need a large space for this game. Each person puts their hands on the shoulders of another, to form a line. The front of the line is now the dragon's head, and that person must try to catch the tail by manoeuvering as the whole line follows.

Dressing-up relay

Ages: **4+** Numbers: **6+**

▶ A relay race with a difference.

Preparation: Each team needs a bag or case filled with large items of clothing.

Put the players into two equal teams and give each one a small suitcase or bag filled with the same amount of all types of clothes – in large sizes, the stranger the better, but all items that children can put on and take off

The Dressing-up relay offers an irresistable combination of running really fast and dressing in bizarre clothes.

themselves. On your signal, the first player in each team puts on all the clothes, runs with the empty suitcase or bag to an agreed place at least 10m (30ft) away, removes the clothing and returns it to the container before running back to their team with the bag of clothes. Each player takes a turn and the winning team is the first to complete the race.

Duck, duck, goose

Ages: **3+** Numbers: **6+**

▶ A lively traditional chasing game.

Preparation: None.

Players sit in a circle. Choose a 'fox', who walks round the outside of the circle, tapping each child on the head and naming them 'duck', until he changes this for one child to 'goose'. The goose must chase the fox around the circle and tag him before he completes a circuit and sits in the goose's place.

If the fox is tagged, he repeats his role. If not, the goose is the new fox.

Variation: The 'fox' becomes the 'dropper', carrying a tissue or handkerchief. They walk round the circle brushing the material over the player's heads and saying, 'Who will I choose? I don't choose you.' At some point they say, 'I choose you' and drop the tissue behind the person's back. That person has to pick up the tissue and chase the dropper to try to avoid taking on the role next time.

Elbow race

Ages: 7+ Numbers: **Any, in pairs**

▶ A race where cooperation is vital.

Preparation: None.

Agree the start and finish line on a forgiving surface such as grass and put the players in pairs, of equal height if possible. Pairs stand back to back and hook their elbows together. They can decide whether one will run forwards while the other runs backwards, or whether to go for a side-by-side approach.

Fan or blow?

Ages: **Any** Numbers: **Any, in pairs**

▶ Which is more powerful, fanning or puffing?

Preparation: A table tennis ball (or a blown egg) and a fan made from paper.

This game works best on carpets or rugs. Mark out the ends of the course on the floor with string or tape and put the ball or egg in the middle. One player kneels behind the line at each end. The aim of the game is to get the ball or egg over the line opposite, but one player has the paper fan and the other can only blow with their mouth.

Variations: 1 If one method is proving too powerful, allow another player to join the weaker side. **2** Use a piece of paper (even a bank note!) as the missile.

Feather hover

Ages: **Any** Numbers: **Any**

▶ Can you keep the feather hovering?

Preparation: One feather.

Players lie on their backs and a feather is thrown into the air. Players can only raise their heads as they blow at the feather to stop it landing on them.

Feather volleyball

Ages: **Any** Numbers: **Any, in equal teams**

▶ A huff and puff version of volleyball.

Preparation: Lay a piece of string across the room, and get a feather.

Each team is positioned either side of the string. The aim of the game is to get the feather to land on the opposing floor. Players are allowed three blows at a time, and can pass to others in their team before sending the feather over the 'net'.

Follow your nose

Ages: **6+** Numbers: **3-8**

▶ A race using your nose.

Preparation: Starting and finishing line, objects to push.

This is a straight race to nudge an object from start to finish line with your nose, so players will be crawling along on hands and knees. You could use ping pong balls or tennis balls, but players will be tempted to push them in front of them. Better ideas are grapes, plastic bricks or toy cars.

Fox and chickens

Ages: **6+** Numbers: **Any**

▶ A much-loved chasing game that needs a lot of space.

Preparation: None.

Choose the first 'chicken' and a 'fox'. The chicken goes to the far side of the space, and calls out the name of any child. They are the next chicken and must try to get across without being caught by the fox. Captured chickens have to stand still while the game continues around them.

Go for the string

Ages: **6**+ Numbers: **Two at a time**

▶ A race to get the prize.

Preparation: Two chairs, some string and a prize.

Place two chairs about 3m (10ft) apart, facing away from each other. Tie a prize, like a bag of sweets or a toy, in the middle of a long piece of string and lay this string so that it runs from under one chair to the other. Players sit in their chairs, then race around their opponent's chair, sit down again and pull the string until they get the prize.

Grapefruit squash

Ages: **7**+ Numbers: **Equal teams**

▶ A pass-the-fruit game using your legs.

Preparation: One grapefruit per team.

In this game the grapefruit is passed through the team. They start by lying side by side, and the grapefruit is placed on the first player's ankles, from where it must be transferred without the use of hands at any time.

Variation: Try this with balloons or oranges.

Headrest

Ages: **8**+ Numbers: **Teams of equal numbers**

▶ A relay race requiring patience and strong neck muscles.

Preparation: Inflated balloon or beach ball for each team.

Choose two or three teams of equal numbers. Agree a race course that each team must walk with the balloon balanced on their head. If it drops, they have to let it land, then pick it up and replace it.

Variations: 1 Turn the course into an obstacle race. **2** The balloon must be held between the knees, or batted in the air.

The incredible bulk

Ages: **5+** Numbers: **Any, in teams**

▶ A very silly dressing-up game.

Preparation: Lots of inflated balloons (or get the players to inflate them during the game), plus a large shirt and pair of trousers per team.

The aim of this game is for one member of each team to be wearing the most balloons. They put on the baggy clothes, and the rest of the team starts stuffing in the balloons. Allow two minutes (or the duration of a song) and then count the balloons. Burst balloons count for nothing!

Indoor obstacle race

Ages: **5+** Numbers: **Any**

▶ A popular furniture-climbing activity.

Preparation: Remove anything fragile, and set out the furniture to create a course.

Set out a course that requires going over and under the furniture. Players can either go round it on their own, perhaps being timed to find the fastest, or as a paired race.

Variations: 1 Children travel the obstacle race blindfolded with a helper offering instructions. **2** This is more of a stunt, and you can only do it once. Set up the course, show it to two children who are then blindfolded. While they prepare themselves or are distracted by someone perhaps offering 'helpful' guidance, move the furniture to the middle of the room, or even take some out. Watching them attempt the course in thin air is hilarious.

All fall down

A Victorian party trick, which, like the blind obstacle race, could only be performed once, was called 'Prussian exercises'. In this, a team was lined up and their corporal gave a series of military commands such as saluting and marching before ordering them into the firing position, on their knees with arms outstretched. At this point he nudged the soldier on the end of the line, causing the entire army to tip inelegantly sideways.

Jackets

Ages: **6+** Numbers: **Two at a time**

▶ A dressing and running race.

Preparation: Two jackets, two chairs, some string and a prize.

Turn out the sleeves of two jackets and hang each on the back of a chair. Place the chairs back to back about 2m (6ft) apart, with a length of string or rope running between them. The players stand on their chair until told to start, then have to put on the jackets with sleeves the right way out, do up any buttons, race round the other chair and pull on the string.

Jugglers

Ages: 4+ Numbers: **Any**

▶ A test of skill.

Preparation: An inflated balloon or beach ball for each player.

This is a simple contest to see who can keep the balloon up in the air for the longest. However, the good thing about this game is that you can set any of these rules:

▶ Use feet only.

▶ Use hands only.

▶ Use the nose only.

▶ Stand on one leg.

▶ Clap after each hit of the balloon.

Keeping a balloon in the air is a full-time job.

Mind your back

Ages: **Any** Numbers: **Two players at a time**

▶ A positioning game that is fun to watch.

Preparation: Pieces of paper with numbers written on them quite large, safety pins.

A pair of players each has a number pinned to his back, and stands in the middle of a circle formed by the guests. The aim of the game is to spot your opponent's number while concealing yours. No contact is allowed.

Obstacle and skills race

Ages: **6**+ Numbers: **Any**

▶ A sports' day classic.

Preparation: Sports equipment such as balls, beanbags, rackets, etc.

With a bit of imagination you can make a pretty good obstacle race and tie it in with your party theme. Children can crawl under old sheets (peg them loosely to the ground), jump over canes resting on buckets, etc. Put in a skills section too, like balancing a ball on a bat, or bouncing a rugby ball.

Variation: Run the race in teams as a relay.

The tension builds up and up in the game of Packet pickup. This picture shows one technique for picking up the packet; page 74 shows another.

Packet pickup

Ages: **6**+ Number: **Any**

▶ A test of flexibility for young and old.

Preparation: An empty cereal box.

Put the empty cereal box in the middle of the circle, open side up. Each child in turn has to pick up the box with their

teeth, without touching it or the floor with their hands or legs. After each round, tear a strip from the top of the box, making the stretch required longer. The winner is the one who can stoop the lowest.

Pinball

Ages: **5**+ Numbers: **Any**

▶ A frenetic ball-bashing game.

Preparation: A soft ball.

Everyone stands in a circle facing outwards, feet set wide apart so that they touch those of the neighbouring people. Players bend down to swing their arms between their legs. One person goes into the middle and a ball is released into the circle. The aim of the game is to bash the ball to hit the person in the middle, who will try to dodge it. If they get hit, another player takes a turn.

Variations: 1 Try this with a balloon. **2** Use two balls. **3** Reverse the game by asking the player in the middle to get the ball out through the legs of the people in the circle.

Pinball is a hectic game not for the faint-hearted or the stiff-backed.

Ping pong relay

Ages: 5+ Numbers: **Equal teams**

▶ A fun race using table tennis balls.

Preparation: One straw per player, plus one table tennis ball per pair.

Put the players into teams, half of each at each end of the room. Using a straw, the players must blow ping pong balls across the room to their teammate, who then blows it back. Players must travel on all fours as they follow their ball. Use a permanent market pen to put a different colour or symbol on each ball so that they can't get mixed up.

Variation: Try using a slightly bigger but light ball.

Red light, green light

Ages: 3+ Numbers: **Any**

▶ A popular playground game.

Preparation: Mark or use two parallel lines to define the middle space.

All players stand behind one of the lines, apart from the Police Officer, who stands with his back to them, calls 'Green light' and counts to ten in his head (or aloud). Players move across the space until he shouts 'Red light' and turns round. All players must freeze, and if the Police Officer sees anyone move, they have to go back to the starting line. First across the other line wins.

Red lion

Ages: 6+ Numbers: **Any**

▶ A lively tagging game.

Preparation: None.

One player is the lion, another is his keeper. They stand in one place while the other players taunt the lion by calling 'Red lion, red lion, come out of your den.

Anybody you catch will be one of your men' until the keeper cries 'Loose' and the lion is let out to try to catch someone. If he grabs someone and roars 'Red lion' three times before they can pull away, they become a lion too and the animals retreat to their den for play to re-start. As the game proceeds, new rules are introduced. If the keeper calls 'Cow catcher', the lions must join hands and trap someone between them. If the yell is 'Doubles', lions must hunt arm-in-arm in pairs, but still grab their victims. A shout of 'Tight' means all lions must join hands and surround their prey. The player who evades the big cats longest wins.

Sharp elbows

Ages: **8+** Numbers: **Any**

▶ A polite wrestling match, which can get a bit rough if you're not careful.

Preparation: Prize or prizes.

This might not be a game for frail grannies. Put everyone in a circle, facing outwards and with elbows hooked with their neighbour's. Put a prize such as a £5 note, or a fizzy drink, in the centre of the circle. The aim of the game is to get that prize, but the whole circle has to stay linked by the arms.

Sleeping bag race

Ages: **4+** Numbers: **Any**

▶ A variation on an old sports' day favourite, perfect for sleepovers.

Preparation: Sleeping bag for each person.

This is just a sack race, but the competitors are zipped inside their own sleeping bags. Play on a safe surface (perhaps play mats or airbeds).

Splat!

Ages: **7+** Numbers: **16+**

▶ A fast-moving game for large groups.

Preparation: None.

Everyone stands in a circle with one player in the middle. They turn and blindly fire an imaginary custard pie at someone, calling 'Splat!'. The victim sits down and the two players either side race to be first to 'splat' the other. So play proceeds with fewer players and the gaps between them grow. When two players remain, they come to the middle and stand back to back. The original 'Splatter' now chooses a category such as colours and says them, one at a time. Each time they hear a word in the category, the two players take a step forward, away from each other, but when the caller says a word not in the category, they race to turn and deliver the final, winning 'Splat!'.

If you can't agree who 'splatted' first, call it a draw and continue the game.

Spud

Ages: **6+** Numbers: **Any**

▶ An old, fast-moving throwing game.

Preparation: Suitable outdoor playing area, soft ball.

One player has the ball and the others must gather round him until he starts to count to ten, whereupon they scatter. When he stops counting, all freeze and the ball thrower is allowed four giant strides in any direction (one for each letter of 'spud' – some players like to chant each letter as they step). He now throws the ball at another player (aiming below the head). If they catch it, play starts as before. If not, they get the letter 'S' – next time it will be 'P', then 'U' and if they reach 'D', they are out. If you play long enough, there will be only two players left, but you can stop anytime.

Variation: Instead of counting to ten to start the game, the player throws the ball in the air and calls out the name of another player. If that person catches it, they throw it up and call another name. If it is not caught, the named person takes on the role of thrower.

Stitch up

Ages: **6+** Numbers: **Any**

▶ A race in a circle that requires a quick-minded runner.

Preparation: None.

All players stand slightly apart in a circle, apart from two left outside: the 'stitcher' and the chaser, who start on opposite sides. The chaser (who must stay outside the circle) starts to run after the 'stitcher', who is allowed to run inside the circle as long as he exits quickly. If he runs straight through, nothing changes, but if he 'weaves' by leaving via the gap next to where he entered, the two players he first ran between as he entered join hands and the gap is 'stitched up' and blocked. If the stitcher manages to end the game inside a stitched up circle, he wins. If he is tagged before this, new players take on the two running roles.

Story game

Ages: 4+ Numbers: **12+**

▶ A listening and running game.

Preparation: Chair at far end of room.

Agree a familiar story, such as 'Red Riding Hood'. Allocate characters so that you have several 'Big bad wolves', 'Red Riding Hoods' and so on. Tell the story, and whenever their character is mentioned, that player must run to the end of the room, round the chair and back. You can add touches to the story to keep them guessing about who must run next.

Streets and alleys

Ages: 7+ Numbers: **15+**

▶ A tag game where everyone plays their part.

Preparation: None.

You need an indoor or outdoor area large enough for the players to stand facing the same way in rows and columns to form a grid, with enough space for others to run between them, but close enough to join hands. They must do this so they create rows (known as 'streets') for other players to run down. Three players stay off the grid: the caller, runner and chaser. The runner zooms along the 'streets' with a head start ahead of the chaser. When the caller shouts 'alleys', players let go of the hand they are holding, turn to their right and join up instead with the person to the side, so that the streets are turned at right angles into alleys. In this way the caller can make life easier, or harder, for the runner and chaser as they have to keep changing direction.

Sweetie balance

Ages: 4+ Numbers: **Any**

▶ Everybody wins playing this slow, calm game.

Preparation: Bag of small wrapped sweets.

Everyone lies on their back while you place a wrapped sweet

on their nose or forehead. Call out movements such as 'touch your nose' or 'put your feet in the air'. If the sweet falls off, they get to eat it. The winner is the last one still balancing a sweet, winning a prize.

Tag
Ages: **5+** Numbers: **Any**
▶ A game children have played for thousands of years.
Preparation: None.
One child is 'it', and must catch the others by touching them, in which case they become fellow catchers until there is one child left. They start the next game.
Variations: 1 Anyone who is tagged must 'freeze', but can be released by other children tapping them, or squeezing through their legs (this variation is called 'Stuck in the mud'). Anyone tagged three times becomes a catcher. **2** Anyone tagged has to join hands with the tagger and work with them to tag other players. When there are four in the chain, it separates into two

watch out!

Tag

Make it clear how players should be tagged so that they can't get hurt – for example a light tap on both hips. Demonstrate this and get the particularly competitive children to show you how they will tag painlessly and safely.

pairs. **3** Only allow tagging on certain body parts, such as elbows or feet. The tagger changes the body part frequently. **4** Tagged players have to put a hand over their 'wound' where they were touched. The other hand must cover a second wound. When they have three wounds, they join the tagger. **5** Players run with their arms hooked to make a pair. They cannot be tagged but there is a single 'runner' who is the target for the tagger. If the 'runner' links arms with a pair, the person on the other side becomes the 'runner'. **6** Tag by jumping on someone's shadow (this needs a sunny day and a watchful referee!). **7** Tag by attaching clothes pegs to clothes. **8** Have 'safety zones' such as trees or poles, where players cannot be tagged. **9** Everybody has to run backwards, or skip or hop. **10** Play in the dark, give the tagger a torch and they tag by naming whoever they recognise when they shine light on them.

Tangle

Ages: **6+** Numbers: **8 or more**

▶ Unravel the human chain.

Preparation: None.

With one person out of the room, everybody joins hands in a circle, then starts ducking under arms, stepping over legs, turning the circle into a tangle of bodies, without letting go of any hands. Then everyone shuffles towards the middle to tighten the knot. In comes the untangler to unravel the puzzle without separating any hands. If you want to do it as a competition, time how long it takes to get everyone back into a circle, or divide into teams.

Three-ball relay

Ages: **6+** Numbers: **Equal teams**

▶ A tricky relay race.

Preparation: An agreed course, plus three different balls for each team.

Give each team three balls – they can be different sizes (for example you could use a tennis ball, a rugby ball and a beach ball). On your signal, the first child in each team runs the course, rolling the three balls as they go. They can only touch the balls with their hands. When they complete the course they pass the three balls on to the next player, and so on.

Variation: Balls must be kicked.

Three-legged race

Ages: **6+** Numbers: **Any, in pairs**

▶ A traditional sports' day favourite for outdoors.

The Three-ball relay is a tricky challenge testing judgement and coordination.

Preparation: Strips of soft material for tying legs together.

This is a well-loved game where two people have to run with their adjacent legs tied together (use soft fabric rather than string for this to avoid rope burns). **Variation:** Add a third person to each team and have a four-legged race.

Ticket man

Ages: **6+** Numbers: **8+**

▶ A lively seat-swapping game that needs some preparation.

Preparation: Have a set of places (they could be postcards or just pieces of paper with the word on) and a list of these with some extras thrown in.

Give all but one of the players a place name or postcard. Everyone sits in a chair in the circle apart from the 'ticket man' who stands in the middle, holding the list. He calls out two places, and the players holding them have to swap seats before the ticket man can sit in the empty seat. Whoever is left standing is the next ticket man.

Variation: Use animal pictures instead of place names.

Toes

Ages: **6+** Numbers: **Any, in pairs**

▶ An unusual paired rolling activity that can be done as a race.

Preparation: None, but you need a large area with a forgiving surface such as grass or a carpet.

Get everyone to practise lying on the floor or ground facing away from a partner, but with the toes touching. Now the pair must roll (agree the direction first!). This can serve as a game in itself as you can measure how fair each pair can travel. If there is room, pairs can race each other to a finishing line.

Triangular tug of war

Ages: **6+** Numbers: **3, or groups of 3**

▶ An unusual tug of war.

Preparation: Tie a rope into a loop. You also need three handkerchiefs.

Each player pulls on the rope, forming a triangle shape. When the rope is taut, a handkerchief is placed 1m (3ft) behind each player. Players tug on the rope until they can reach down to pick up the handkerchief.

Ultimate

Ages: **8+** Numbers: **Two equal teams (7–10 each side works well)**

▶ A disc-throwing team game that is very popular in the USA.

Preparation: Large outdoor playing area, and a plastic disc (also known as a frisbee).

Agree the dimensions of the pitch (a football or rugby pitch is ideal). Teams line up at opposite ends of the pitch. Agree which team will receive first, and throw them the disc. The rules are like a blend of football and rugby:

▶ The aim of the game is to throw the disc to a teammate standing over the opponent's goal line.

▶ No one can run with the disc: it is moved by throwing.

▶ Players without the disc can go anywhere.

▶ There is no contact at all.

▶ Passes can be in any direction.

▶ A team retains possession of the disc by catching it. If it hits the ground, possession goes to the opposition.

▶ Players can intercept any pass. If they touch the disc at all, possession goes to their team.

▶ If the disc goes out of play, the opposition throw it in from that point.

'Goals' are scored by passing to one of your own players standing behind the opposing goal line, after which play restarts with the opposing team in possession.

Volleyball

Ages: 7+ Numbers: **Equal teams**

▶ A highly competitive team game.

Preparation: High net and balloon or beach ball.

Set up a high net (a washing line will do) and have two teams play volleyball over it with balloons.

Variations: 1 Put players into pairs, each with a towel. One side launches a balloon one-third filled with water over the net, for the other team to catch in their towel and return. If the balloon bursts, they lose. **2** Play 'one team volleyball' where the whole team has to cross back and forth after the balloon.

Wacky races

Ages: 4+ Numbers: **Any**

▶ Silly ideas for racing.

Preparation: A few ideas of variations on the races.

This can be played individually or as a relay. You just have to think of silly (but safe) ways for the competitors to run, like with their hands on their heads, or sidestepping, balancing a toy on their head, in pairs with one leg tied together, backwards, while singing a song, and get them to do it. Have a few ideas ready and then ask the children what else you could do: they'll have lots of suggestions!

Walk the plank

Ages: **5+** Numbers: **Any**

▶ A balancing game that gets harder and harder.

Preparation: A plank or board about 2m (6ft) long.

The board is put on the floor and players just have to walk it without stepping into the 'sea'. Over the following rounds make up increasingly difficult handicaps: walk backwards, hopping, with hands round ankles, passing an obstacle placed in the middle, looking through binoculars backwards, blindfolded, and finally: any combination of these!

Variation: Try using rope instead of a plank.

Walk the plank is a fun balancing test that is also perfect for pirate-themed parties.

Wall game

Ages: **6**+ Numbers: **4**+

▶ A throwing and catching game with a twist.

Preparation: A ball and a suitable wall.

Each player is given a number. The first player throws the ball against the wall while calling out one of these numbers. Whoever has that number must catch the ball after one bounce, and play continues. Each successful catch scores one. Players do not score if the ball bounces twice, unless it is agreed that the throw was not fair, in which case the throw is repeated.

Water and spoon race

Ages: **5**+ Numbers: **Any, in teams**

▶ A water-carrying race.

Preparation: A bowl, glass and spoon for each player.

Place a large bowl filled with water at one end of the space, and one empty plastic glass for each team at the other. Players race to fill the glass with water from the bowl, transporting the liquid with a spoon.

Variations: 1 If you can colour the water with food dye, so much the better. **2** Use raisins or sweets instead of water.

Wheelbarrow race

Ages: **6**+ Numbers: **Any, in pairs**

▶ A traditional children's race for outdoors or a forgiving surface.

Preparation: None.

This is a straight race where one of the pair walks on their hands, their legs being held by their partner behind them.

Whose race?

Ages: **6**+ Numbers: **Any**

▶ A race where you have to listen well.

Preparation: Two cones about 4m (12ft) apart.

The challenger stands by one cone, all other players behind the other. The challenger calls out a category, like 'cars' or 'animals'. Each player chooses one item in that category and whispers it to the leader, who then calls out all the words to the challenger. He selects one and shouts it. Whoever said that word must now race to get round the opposite cone and back before the challenger does the same from his cone. Whoever loses is the next challenger.

Your turn

Ages: 5+ Numbers: **Any, in teams**

▶ A team race that can be as silly as you like.

Preparation: An inflated balloon or beach ball for each team. An agreed zone for each team, and a timer.

This is a series of challenges for teams who must stop their balloon from hitting the floor. Each team has one balloon, which they must pat into the air as many times as they can in one minute. However, no player can hit the balloon twice in a row: and the whole team must be involved as much as possible (so two players can pat it between them). Teams keep a count of how many times they hit the balloon in one minute and you score accordingly.

Variations: 1 The balloon can only be touched with the head, feet, elbows or fists. **2** The team must kneel to play. **3** Have a race to be the first to complete 20 touches of the balloon. **4** Put a tablespoon of water into the balloons before inflating to weigh them down slightly.

5 Musical games

We all respond to music. It is a great way to add atmosphere, and musical games have their own sense of occasion. These games do not require superb singing voices or, in many cases, any singing at all. They do tend to be fairly lively and demand a lot of involvement. Incidentally, music can supply the timing element to any game that needs a clear beginning and end.

Musical games

In this section there are wonderful traditional musical games such as Musical chairs and Musical statues, but also acting activites such as Blind conductor and, of course, many opportunities for someone to sing the show-stopper.

Arches

Ages: **6+** Numbers: **10+, in pairs**

▶ A dancing game that must have been played for centuries.

Preparation: Have music ready.

Players pair up, and two pairs are invited to join raised hands to form an arch. When the music starts, the other pairs must dance in and out of this arch. When the music stops, down come the arms to trap any pair underneath them. Those players join the arch and play continues until there are no dancers left.

Balloon dance

Ages: **6+** Numbers: **Pairs**

▶ A dance that goes with a bang.

It's tricky enough keeping the balloon in place without having to follow a rhythm!

Preparation: Have music ready. Inflated balloons.

Each pair faces each other, holding the balloon between their chests. They must dance when the music is playing and stop when it stops. Pairs are 'out' if their balloon bursts.

Variations: 1 Give everyone a balloon. Players must find a partner with the same or similar colour balloon (it is up to you if you want to fix this so that couples are mixed). **2** Everyone has a balloon, which is held between their knees. Players now form a circle by holding hands, and they must all dance without losing their balloon.

Beat the music

Ages: **6+** Numbers: **Any**

▶ An elimination game that can get frantic.

Preparation: Have music ready. A cane or stick.

Find a surface that won't be damaged by a stick. Everyone sits in a circle, one person with the cane. When the music starts they must tap the cane on the floor three times and pass it on. The next player does the same, the cane going in the same direction. Whoever has the cane when the music stops is out.

Variation: The cane can be passed in either direction.

Blind conductor

Ages: **6+** Numbers: **Any**

▶ A lively singing game with chances for solos!

Preparation: Blindfold and 'baton'.

Appoint your conductor, who should be blindfolded and given a baton, which could be a pencil or something jokey such as a long balloon. Everyone moves in a circle around the conductor, singing or humming an agreed tune as he waves his baton. When he stops waving, everyone is silent. Then he points at someone, who must continue singing, disguising their voice if they wish. If the conductor guesses who it is they swap places. If not, the game starts again.

Find your partner

Ages: **6+** Numbers: **10+, in equal numbers**

▶ A good, active warm-up game.

Preparation: Have music ready.

Put the players into pairs, and then organize them so there is an inner circle of children, each facing their partner, who is in an outer circle. When the music starts, each circle turns in the opposite direction to the other (agree this first!). When it stops, players race to pair up with their partner.

Hats

Ages: **5+** Numbers: **10+**

▶ A lively circle game.

Preparation: Have music ready, plus a selection of hats.

Everyone sits in a circle, all except one wearing a hat. When the music starts, players pass the hats on. When it stops, they put on the hat, and the hatless player is out. Remove another hat and start the next round.

How do I look?

Ages: **5+** Numbers: **Any**

▶ A lively dressing-up game.

Preparation: Have music ready. A wide range of large clothing in a bag.

Everyone sits in a circle, passing round the bag until the music stops. Whoever is then holding the bag must put on something from it. Play continues until there is no more clothing, when you can then decide who looks the silliest. Raid your local charity shop for outlandish and large outfits for this game.

Musical balloons

Ages: **5+** Numbers: **6+**

▶ A balloon version of musical chairs.

Preparation: Have music ready. Plenty of inflated balloons or beach balls.

Blow up enough balloons for all but one of the players. When the music starts, players must pat the balloons in the air. When it stops, they catch a balloon, and one person will be 'out'. Continue until you have a winner.

Musical bingo

Ages: **6**+ Numbers: **10**+

▶ Dance your way to the prize!

Preparation: Have music ready. Prizes, numbered tickets and a numbered dancing area.

Mark out large (about 1m/3ft) squares on the dancing area with chalk or tape, and number each one with a sticky label (make sure it can't be rubbed off by busy feet). Players dance while you play music, moving between the squares. When you stop the music, everyone should quickly get into one of the squares, so you can draw the raffle ticket and award the prize. If no one is standing in that square, draw again. If there are two people in it, neither gets a prize.

Musical chairs

Ages: **3**+ Numbers: **6**+

▶ A traditional lively racing game.

Preparation: Have music ready. Chairs.

Make a line of chairs, each slightly apart facing the opposite direction to its neighbour. Each player stands by a chair. When you play the music, players must march in the same direction around the chairs. While it plays, remove one chair. When you stop the music, everybody sits down in the nearest chair, leaving one person 'out'. Continue until two players race to sit in the one remaining chair.

Variations: 1 Have two rows of back-to-back chairs, or chairs in a circle. Put the chairs into two separate circles and tell the players

Musical chairs has been a party staple for years, but there are plenty of variations to bring new interest.

they must walk in a figure of eight around these. **2** Pillows, cushions or large sheets of paper can be used instead of chairs. **3** Use items of clothing or hats that people must put on instead of sitting down. **4** Players walk around a pile of balloons, and pick one up when the music stops. **5** Tape an inflated balloon to the seat of each chair. Players pop them when they sit down. (You'll need a large supply of balloons – it could be one way to get rid of any you used as decorations.) **6** Each player must walk elegantly round the room with a book balanced on their head. When the music stops they must gently go down on one knee and hold their pose until it starts again. Wobbling or (horror of deportment horrors) dropping the book result in instant expulsion.

Musical statues
Ages: **3–9** Numbers: **6+**
▶ A 'catch you out' game.
Preparation: Have music ready.

Players have to move about and dance to the music, but must freeze into a statue pose as soon as it stops. Anyone who moves when there is no music is out, and could help you judge the next round.
Variations: 1 When the music stops it is a race to sit on the floor. **2** When the music stops everybody has to stand on one foot, or have one hand on the floor.

Name that tune
Ages: **6+** Numbers: **6+**
▶ A song recognition game.
Preparation: Selection of songs that most of your guests are likely to recognize.

This game is fun in teams of mixed ages. Collect songs suitable for your guests, so have plenty of nursery rhymes for young children, pop hits for teenagers, and so on. You could record them onto tape or burn a disc with them, but otherwise just collect them as CDs or in another format and conceal any packaging that identifies them. Play a short burst from the start of the song and invite guesses as to what it is. Keep doing this until it is identified. You could give extra marks for speed or for naming the artist, or stating the year it was made.

Variations: 1 Write out some lyrics and read them for players to guess. **2** Tape songs and jingles from TV and radio stations. **3** Turn it into a miming contest. **4** Play karaoke recordings of songs without the words.

Next line

Ages: **6+** Numbers: **Any, in teams**

▶ A test of how carefully you listen.

Preparation: A selection of reasonably well-known songs appropriate to your guests.

Play the song until the first line is sung, then stop the music and invite teams to guess (or sing, for extra points) the next line.

Variation: Don't play the music, just read out the lyrics. This really is much harder.

Numbers

Ages: **6+** Numbers: **10+**

▶ A lively ice-breaking game.

Preparation: Have music ready.

Everyone dances or marches while the music is playing, but when it stops, the leader calls out a number. Everyone has to get into a group of that number. Anyone not in a group is 'out'.

Variations: 1 Instead of numbers, call out shapes for groups to make. **2** Put players in teams and call out letters of the alphabet for them to form.

Pass the hoop

Ages: **6+** Numbers: **6+**

▶ A plastic hoop-passing game.

Preparation: Two large plastic hula hoops. Have music ready.

Everyone stands in a circle, holding hands. Thread the two hula hoops onto the arms of two different players. When the music starts, players must

Pass the hoop calls for flexible joints and a lot of teamwork.

pass the hoop around the circle while never letting go of their neighbours' hands. They will have to step and duck through the hoop. Whoever is 'wearing' a hoop when the music stops is out. **Variation:** If you have enough players for two teams, this could become a race to get the hoop through the whole team.

Pass the parcel

Ages: **3**+ Numbers: **6**+

▶ A lively traditional party game.
Preparation: A present loosely wrapped in many layers of paper (newspaper is fine). Allow about one layer per person. Have music ready.

Play some music while the children pass the parcel round. Whenever you stop it, the child holding the parcel removes a layer of wrapping, until the present is revealed.

Variations: 1 Place a small gift in each layer, so more people get a prize. **2** Write forfeits on slips of paper and put one between each layer. **3** Tell children to close their eyes while the parcel is being passed. Then they have the fun of seeing who has it when the music stops. **4** The parcel must be passed behind their backs. **5** Turn the game into 'Eat the parcel' by putting a sweet between each layer. You could even use edible rice paper for some of the layers! **6** Players pass a balloon to each other behind their backs. When the music stops, whoever has the balloon is out of the game.

Rug rumba

Ages: **6**+ Numbers: **10**+

▶ A musical elimination game.

Preparation: A rug. Have music ready.

Everyone forms a circle, with at least one of them standing on the rug. When the music starts, everyone must march or dance around in a circle, passing over the rug. Anyone who is caught on the rug when the music stops is out.

Singing bingo

Ages: **8+** Numbers: **10+**

▶ A very funny singing game.

Preparation: Sets of tickets numbered 1–20.

Warn all players that they must think of five different songs that they can sing at least part of. Now give everyone five of the numbered tickets (or they can write their own choice of numbers up to 20), and put one set of numbers in a bag. Draw a number and call it out. Everyone with that number must now sing their song, even if this means repeatedly singing the first line. Stop them after about 20 seconds and draw the next number. Keep going until someone has sung five times – players can challenge if they do not think five different songs were sung.

Variations: 1 At Christmas parties, all songs must be carols. **2** Award prizes for best or worst singing, loudest solo, etc.

Songdraw

Ages: **6+** Numbers: **Teams of four or five**

▶ Can you describe a song in a picture?

Preparation: Cards on which you write the titles of songs that everyone is likely to have heard of.

Put the players into teams and give them pencil and paper. One person from each team comes to you to look at the card (you can whisper the title if necessary), then returns to draw the title for their team to guess by singing the song. First team to guess correctly wins each round.

Variation: The song list can reflect the time of year, like Christmas carols.

must know

Fair play
In any game where music is played and stopped to give players a go, it is vital that you play fair, and are seen to play fair. You could turn your back and leave things to chance, but people will think if very unjust if someone gets two goes while others miss out. One way round this is to 'manage' the music so that a different person gets a turn each time, until the final round, when you turn round and let fate take its course.

Spoon scramble

Ages: **8**+ Numbers: **10**+

▶ A rather undignified elimination game.

Preparation: Have music ready. Plenty of spoons.

Put out one less spoon than your number of players. On hands and knees, players must dance to the music, grabbing a spoon when it stops. The player without a spoon is out.

Variation: Try playing this game blindfold!

Spot the leader

Ages: **6**+ Numbers: **8**+

▶ An observation game that is very popular with children.

Preparation: Have music ready. Be ready to lead the game yourself.

One player leaves the room to become the guesser. Put some music on and choose one person to lead the others clapping along, but they must change the rhythm regularly, and vary which body part they hit. When the guesser is invited in, they try to work out who is leading the clapping.

Variations: 1 Put players in a circle to make it harder to spot the leader. **2** Instead of clapping, have a dance leader. **3** Everyone has to become a statue, but one person leads them in changing their position.

Children love the chance to star with the tambourine, and the rhythm tapping game calls for careful listeners.

Tambourine game

Ages: **5**+ Numbers: **6**+

▶ A rhythm-tapping game that is fun for large family groups.

Preparation: None.

Demonstrate how you can tap the rhythm of a name, giving one hit per beat or syllable (so Nanny Joan is two hits followed by one). Players tap the rhythm of someone else's full name and everybody has to guess who it is. Get children to whisper the name they will tap to you first so you can help with the rhythm and ensure everyone will know the name.

Variations: 1 Tap the names of pop stars or other famous people (you might need to drop in a clue or two). **2** Tap the names of objects in the room.

To the tune of another

Ages: **8+** Numbers: **Any**

▶ A challenging singing task.

Preparation: Karaoke backing tapes and sets of lyrics.

Ask for a volunteer to sing a song to a backing tape, but give them a set of lyrics to a different, well-known song. The results are often hilarious.

Traffic lights

Ages: **5+** Numbers: **Any**

▶ A fun singing activity.

Preparation: Cut out three paper circles (one green, one orange, one red) and mount them onto card so they look like a traffic light.

This is a way to liven up a singalong. Agree the song to be sung, and when you are pointing at green, everyone sings as usual. However, when you point to the orange 'light', everyone must clap the words instead of singing. Switch to red, and the song continues in people's heads in silence, until you point back to green or orange, at which point they pick up the song where it would have got to if everyone was still singing. Once people are familiar with the rules, this is a lively, fun way of enjoying a song or two together.

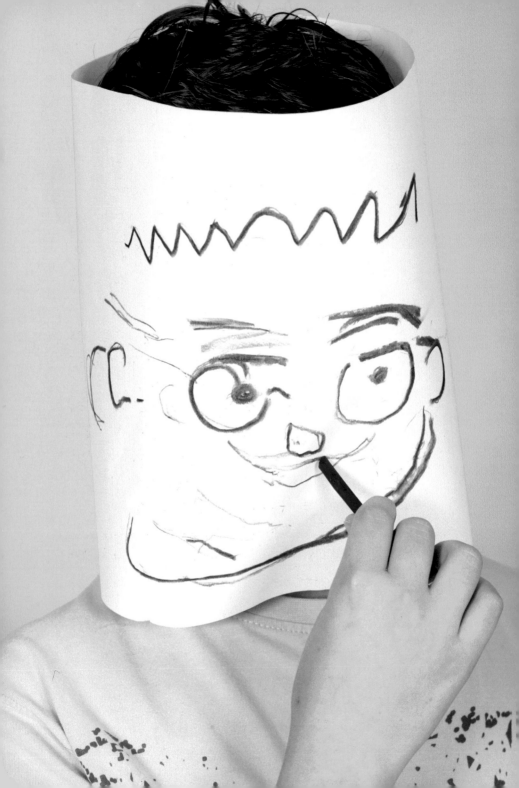

6 Pencil and paper games

Pencil and paper games tend to be fairly quiet and long lasting. Some of these games call for a fair bit of preparation, but regard it as an investment because most stay entertaining for quite a long time. These games offer challenges to individuals but many also give a chance for guests to work in teams. Are you going to set family against family, or divide the group by generation or gender? Whichever you choose, it's bound to get hotly competitive, even if they stay in their seats!

Pencil and paper games

Make sure you have a plentiful supply of pens, pencils and sharpeners, paper and (easily overlooked) something to rest it on. Now you're ready to challenge the skills of even the most ardent crossword lover, and see how quick your guests are on the draw.

Acronyms

Ages: **10+** Numbers: **Any**

▶ A game requiring an inventive mind.

Preparation: Pen and paper for each player. Have a list of words with four letters ready.

An acronym is a sentence where the first letter of each word forms a word itself. For example, GAME is an acronym of Great Achievers Master Exams. The leader supplies the target word, and players or teams have 5 minutes to create an acronym. Marks can be awarded for the funniest or those that match a party theme.

Anagram quiz

Ages: **10+** Numbers: **Any**

▶ A good ice-breaking game.

Preparation: Card or paper with eight-letter objects written on them. Safety pins.

Pin one piece of paper with an eight-letter word written on it to the back of each guest. You can repeat words. They walk around asking other guests if there are certain letters in their word. They can only ask one guest at a time and for one letter at a time. When they have all eight letters, they have to work out what the word is.

▶ Suggested words on a party theme: barbeque, carnival, carousel, feasting, festival, jamboree.

Bagface

Ages: **6+** Numbers: **Any**

▶ A tricky face-drawing game (see the photograph on page 118).

Preparation: Large paper bags or sheets and charcoal drawing sticks or felt-tipped pens.

Players put the paper bag or sheet round or over their head, and try to draw their own portrait on it. Get a group to show their drawings and guess whose is whose.

watch out!

Plastic bags
Remind children playing this game that they should never put plastic bags over their heads as it could stop them breathing.

Battleships

Ages: **7+** Numbers: **Any, in two teams**

▶ A giant version of this popular grid game.

Preparation: Pens. Two large ten-by-ten grids drawn on paper.

Label the squares on the horizontal axis in letters and on the vertical axis in numbers (so the bottom left square is A1). Teams then draw on their fleet, which comprises:

▶ One battleship: four squares.

▶ Two cruisers: three squares each.

▶ Three destroyers: two squares each.

▶ Four submarines: one square each.

All occupied squares must be neighbours – you can't divide the destroyer in half.

Teams now take it in turns to 'fire' at the enemy fleet by calling out a grid reference. They mark hits with the appropriate letter or symbol, and misses with a dot. The whole of a vessel must be hit to sink it (so, for example, it takes three hits to sink a cruiser). First team to destroy the entire opposition fleet wins.

Variation: This game is called Word battleships. Instead of putting in vessels, players write an agreed number of words of agreed lengths, with one letter per square, so that the chart looks like a crossword. The same letter can be used for two words if they cross. Players call out the grid reference, and are told the letter that is there, or if it is blank. Players win in the same way by identifying all the words on their opponent's grid.

Describing a drawing is frustratingly difficult and doubly so when the listener is blindfold and trying to copy your idea.

Blind drawing

Ages: **4+** Numbers: **Any**

▶ A simple drawing game that is funny to watch.

Preparation: Blindfolds, pencil and paper.

Blindfold half the guests. Give them pencil and paper and tell them to draw something – it could be an animal, an object, their house, or someone in the room. You could just give them a minute to draw it, or instruct them what part they should put in next, removing their hand between each bit of sketching. The other guests can enjoy watching the drawings appear, then it is their turn.

Blind write

Ages: **8+** Numbers: **Any, in pairs**

▶ A game where you have to guess what you have written.

Preparation: Blindfolds, pencil and paper.

One player is blindfolded and has a pencil and paper. The other guides their hand to write a word. The blindfolded player has to guess what the word is. Allow three guesses. If the word is really tricky, they can remove their blindfold and see if they recognize their own writing!

Cartoon capers

Ages: **6+** Numbers: **Any**

▶ A calm cartoon-drawing activity.

Preparation: Pictures of cartoon characters with bits covered up or cut out. Pens.

Give each player (or group – they can easily share for this game) a picture of a cartoon character with most of the features either covered up or cut out. Ask each player to copy the features they can see and fill in the rest. Give prizes for the most accurate, funniest, cutest, etc.

Categories

Ages: **8+** Numbers: **Any, in teams**

▶ A long-standing word list game that can become very heated.

Preparation: Have some categories ready to suggest. Each team needs pencil and paper.

Agree a list of six categories for words, such as sports, boys' names, girls' names, food, school and colours. Choose any letter from the alphabet, and the team has 4 minutes to write as many words as they can for each category that start with the target letter. For example if the letter was B, some words could be:

▶ Sports: bowling, biking, bodysurfing.
▶ Boys' names: Ben, Brendan, Barney.
▶ Girls' names: Briony, Beatrice, Belinda.
▶ Food: banana, beans, broccoli.
▶ School: bell, biology, board.
▶ Colours: blue, brown, beige.

After 4 minutes, the host asks each team how many words they had (this is to prevent them adding words they hear during the scoring process). Teams

must know

Ideas for categories
Household items
Towns and cities
Countries
Mathematical terms
Terms for a profession, such as plumbing or accountancy
Electrical goods
Makes of car
Clothing
Words of five letters
Words with the target letter somewhere in the word.

then read out their words (which can be challenged) and score a point for each. The team with the lowest score selects one category to change each round. Appoint a referee to settle any disputes – there are bound to be some!

Variation: 1 Duplicated words do not score at all, so teams only get points for words no other team wrote down. **2** Words of six or more letters score double. **3** Teams only have to find one word in each category, at which point they call 'Stop!' and the game is scored from there. This makes the game shorter and livelier.

Celebrity luggage

Ages: **10+** Numbers: **Any**
▶ A chance to make up some clues about famous people.

Preparation: List of suggested celebrities for anyone who gets stuck. Pen and paper.

This can be played individually or in groups. Players have to imagine that they are packing for a celebrity who is going to a desert island. What items in the suitcase offer a clue as to their identity? Players read out the list, and everyone else has to guess who the celebrity is. It is also fun for the list-maker to explain their selections.

Variation: One player leaves the room and the others agree a celebrity to pack for. Each writes an item for the case on a piece of paper and puts it in a bowl. The player returns and reads one piece of paper at a time until they can guess the celebrity. Each player gets a go, with a different celebrity being chosen each time. The player who scores the lowest number of guesses wins.

Consequences

Ages: 7+ Numbers: **Any**

▶ A very funny story-making game.

Preparation: Long strips of paper and pencils.

In this game every player contributes to a series of silly stories. At the top of their paper, everybody writes a male name – it could anyone, from someone in the room to Superman. Then they fold the paper over so the writing can't be seen and pass it on. Now they write a female name, fold over and pass and so on. The order of writing is:

▶ Male name
▶ Female name
▶ Place where they met
▶ He said
▶ She said
▶ What happened
▶ The world said.

When all strips are completed they are mixed up and re-distributed to be read out. Generally a series of running jokes develops so that each round gets funnier as the ideas evolve.

Variations: 1 A simpler version is called 'Emergency consequences'. In this, each player first writes an emergency in the form of a question, such as 'What would you do if someone fell off the roof?' The paper is folded and passed for the next player, who continues to write what they would do about their own emergency, which has of course been passed on. **2** Players compile advertisements for foods or products. The order of writing is: product name, advertising slogan, instructions for use, price, delivery choice and finally how it will change your life for the better.

must know

Consequences
The game of Consequences inspired a word substituting game and book series called Mad Libs in the 1950s. Devised by Leonard Stern and Roger Price, it used short stories with blanks left for the addition of random nouns, verbs or adjectives.

Crosswords

Ages: **8+** Numbers: **5+**

▶ A game where players make their own word grids.

Preparation: Pen and paper.

This game can be played individually or in pairs. Players mark a grid six squares by six. Then each player calls out a letter in turn. Everybody has to put that letter somewhere in their grid before the next letter is called. The aim of the game is to create words reading across or down the grid. When all 36 letters have been called, players score one point per letter of any words they made. Letters cannot be used for two horizontal or vertical words (for example, 'baddy' scores five, and the player cannot also claim points for 'bad' or 'add'). The highest score wins.

Variation: Vary the size of the grid

You don't have to be good at drawing to play most drawing games, but you might need to be fast or lucky.

Die draw

Ages: **6+** Numbers: **Any**

▶ A drawing game that can get really frustrating.

Preparation: Pen, paper and die.

In this game players complete drawings according to what they throw on the die. You need to agree what they must draw. If you have a party theme it could link with it (like 'pirates' – draw a pirate, or 'circuses' – draw a clown). There should be six parts to the drawing, as in this example for a snowman:

▶ Throwing a six means you can start by drawing the body.
▶ Throwing a five means you can add the head.
▶ Throw four to draw the eyes.
▶ Throw three to put in the nose and mouth.
▶ Throw two to add buttons.
▶ Throw one to put on the hat.

The aim of the game is to draw as many 'characters' as you can, but each one must be complete before you can start the next. Set a time limit of, say, 15 minutes and see how many each player has drawn.

Variation: The body has to be drawn in order. So, you have to throw a six first to draw the body, and then a five to add the head, and so on.

Doublets

Ages: **10+** Numbers: **Any**

▶ A very old word-changing game.

Preparation: Pen and paper. Have some examples of doublets to explain the idea.

Players are given a word that they must turn into another specified word with the same number of letters, changing one letter at a time and always making a recognized word. For example, you can turn love to hate like this:

LOVE

HOVE

HAVE

HATE

You can also turn a cat into a dog:

CAT

COT

COG

DOG

The words can be three, four or five letters long. You could set a first word and target word (like cat into dog), or set a first word and ask if they can turn it into a word with opposite meaning, like head into tail. The winner is whoever used the fewest words.

Variation: You can allow players to re-arrange the letter order, so that for example icon becomes coin.

Draw round me

Ages: **3+** Numbers: **9+**

▶ A good warm-up activity.

Preparation: Large sheets of paper and plenty of crayons or felt-tipped pens.

Put the players into teams of three or four. Give each team a large piece of paper (a length of wallpaper lining is perfect) and some crayons or felt-tipped pens. Send each team to a different part of the house and ask them to draw round one person, then colour in the features and clothes. When everyone returns, other teams guess who was the model.

Drawing consequences

Ages: **7+** Numbers: **Any**

▶ A drawing version of the popular game of Consequences (see page 125).

Preparation: Fold sheets of A4 paper lengthways in half and half again so that the creases create strips going across. Felt-tipped pens.

Sit the players in a circle and tell them they are going to draw something (e.g. an alien, an animal or person). Give each of them felt-tipped pens and a sheet of paper. Tell them to draw the head first, drawing the lines of the neck going over the top crease. Then they fold what they have drawn back out of view and pass the sheet on.

The next player draws the shoulders and arms using the neck lines as a guide, folds and passes. Next comes the body (waistline going below the next crease), and finally the legs.

Now they can open up the pictures and see what they look like.

Variation: Fold the paper so that it has five creases, making six strips.

must know

Fun timing
If the game requires players to write or think for about 2 minutes, find a piece of music of that length. It will fill the gap and the silence, and is a less threatening timing method than a ticking clock or someone staring at a stopwatch.

The fame game

Ages: **10+** Numbers: **Any, in teams**

▶ A popular quiz round that can keep people engrossed for ages.

Preparation: A sheet of numbered photocopied photographs of celebrities.

This game requires a lot of preparation but is one that people of all ages enjoy, and is particularly good for creating conversation round the table as people wait for their food. The photocopied sheet should have copies of pictures of a variety of famous people – and it is always fun to include one of the host or other person present taken when they were young. Teams have to identify as many celebrities as they can.

Variation: Cut up the photographs so that the players have to reassemble and then identify the famous people.

Feeling game

Ages: **8**+ Numbers: **Any**

▶ An old favourite game relying on our sense of touch.

Preparation: Several numbered bags containing different objects. Pen and paper.

Put a variety of household objects into different bags (pillowcases will be fine), numbering each bag (or identifying it by colour) and keeping a list of the contents. Players must guess what the objects in the bags are by feeling them, writing or drawing their ideas on a piece of paper. Then you can reveal the contents as they mark their sheets to discover who identified the most. If you have no bags, use a large cardboard box with a hole in the side.

Variation: Blindfold all players, who are in a circle. Give each player one object, which they must feel and pass on. Hide the objects, remove the blindfolds and each player must write down as many of the objects they felt as possible.

Getting people to paint while wearing an oven glove takes the most sophisticated artist back to the nursery!

Glove painting

Ages: **4**+ Numbers: **Any**

▶ A painting competition with a difference.

Preparation: A glove for each player, plus paper, paints and brushes.

All players are asked to paint a picture with the same things in it (for example a house with a chimney, five windows and a door, with a dog in the garden). Painters must wear the glove provided and must use that hand (so you can handicap the better artists by forcing them to paint with their wrong hand). The picture that best incorporates the instructions wins.

Heads and tails

Ages: **10+** Numbers: **Any**

▶ A tricky word-finding game.

Preparation: A few examples of what you are looking for. Pen and paper.

This game can be played individually or in groups. Players have 10 minutes to find words of four or more letters that begin and end with the same letter. Examples are noun, minim, local, gurgling, dead, bomb. Don't allow plural nouns (too easy with all those 's's). Award a point for each word.

Variations: 1 Words of six or more letters score double.
2 Duplicated words score nothing. **3** How about finding words with the same two letters (called digraphs) at each end? Examples are church, decide and tomato.

How many layers, or
handfuls or pairs are
in that jar? Oh, just
take a guess!

How many?

Ages: **6+** Numbers: **Any**

▶ A classic guessing game popular at occasions such as fetes.

Preparation: Jars or bowls of small items such as sweets, beads or pasta shells. Pen and paper.

Players simply write down their estimate of how many items are in each container. Nearest guess wins... the contents!

Variation: If players are guessing on a number of containers, you could score three points for nearest guess, two for second and one for third, and have aggregate scores.

Keyword

Ages: **10+** Numbers: **Any, individually or in teams**

▶ A game requiring logical thought.

Preparation: Pen and paper.

Each player or team creates their own keyword, all of which must have the same number of letters (four is best, but younger players will find three easier). These must be written down and handed to a referee to prevent anyone being tempted to cheat and change their word. Players (or teams) take it in turns to ask any other player if the keyword has any of the letters in a certain word, which must be the same length. They must reply accurately how many of those letters are in the keyword. If letters are repeated, they count twice, so for example if the keyword is BABY and someone guesses BILL, the answer is 'Two letters', because there are two 'B's. If a player correctly identifies another's keyword, he scores a point.

Kim's game

Ages: **6+** Numbers: **Any**

▶ A classic memory game.

Preparation: A tray containing 20 small everyday objects, plus a cloth. Pens and paper.

Bring in the tray filled with items of all shapes and sizes, such as a matchbox, a corkscrew, a candle, including some on top of each other, such as a drawing pin on a saucer. Everyone studies the tray for 1 minute before you remove or cover it and distribute pens and paper. Now they have 5 minutes to write down everything they saw, after which players can mark each other's papers. The one who remembered the most wins.

did you know?

Kim's game
Founder of the Scout movement, Robert Baden-Powell, encouraged the playing of this game to help train the memory. It was named after the main character in the book *Kim* by Rudyard Kipling – a writer Baden-Powell admired. In the book, wannabe spy Kim trains himself to spot tiny details..

Variations: 1 Have the tray brought in by an extravagantly dressed and accessorized assistant. After they leave with the tray, ask players to write everything the assistant was wearing. **2** After the studying period, the host takes the tray out of the room and removes one item. The winner is the first person to identify the missing object.

Kim's game has been enduringly popular for well over a century.

Lines

Ages: 7+ Numbers: **Up to 8**

▶ A strategic line-drawing game.

Preparation: Piece of paper with six rows of six dots marked and pen.

On each turn in this game the player draws a line vertically, horizontally or diagonally to connect one or more dots. After the first go, subsequent turns must start from one end of the last line drawn. The aim of the game is to draw the last possible line on the grid.

Longest word

Ages: 7+ Numbers: **Any, individually or in teams**

▶ A word-making challenge.

Preparation: A few long words to suggest, pen and paper.

Each player or team has the same long word, from which they must make as many new words of three or more letters as they can. Set a time limit and score a point for each word, with a bonus for words that contain six or more letters.

Variations: 1 Older players must make words of four or more letters. **2** Offer bonuses for words that match a theme, like 'Christmas'. **3** Duplicated words score nothing. **4** Choose the letters by allowing each player to call out a letter until you have, say, ten. Be sure to have a mix of vowels and consonants.

Make a face

Ages: 4+ Numbers: **Any**

▶ A drawing activity using balloons.

Preparation: Plenty of inflated balloons and felt-tipped pens.

Everybody has a balloon and a felt-tipped pen. They draw the hair on their balloon, then pass it on so that they draw the eyes on the next one, and the nose on the next, and so on. You could tie each balloon to a chair at the dining table.

Variation: Play the game blindfolded.

Make a list

Ages: 7+ Numbers: **6+**

▶ A quick-thinking speaking game.

Preparation: None.

A player chooses a category, such as song titles, sports or colours, then calls out a word that fits the category. Each player in turn has to find a suitable but different word until someone fails and a new category is selected. Decide from the start whether players can be 'out' or not.

Variations: 1 As well as finding words, players have to clap and snap their fingers in a set rhythm. This keeps everybody involved all the time. **2** Allow players to throw a ball to determine who has to find the next word.

Odd socks

Ages: **7+** Numbers: **6+**

▶ A good ice-breaking game.

Preparation: Ask guests to wear one wrong thing. A sheet with a list of those present may be useful. Pens and paper.

Your invitation should ask guests to come wearing something odd or wrong, such as odd socks, unmatched earrings, trousers back to front. Guests have to note down the other players 'errors' as they mingle.

Paint a portrait

Ages: **3+** Numbers: **Any**

▶ A drawing and guessing game.

Preparation: Slips of paper with the name of a guest on each one and pens and paper.

Hand out the slips of paper folded up so no one sees what others get. Give them 10 minutes to draw or paint a portrait of that person – without looking at them too obviously. Then everyone holds up their pictures and the others guess who is who.

Variation: No hands can be used: paint with the feet only!

Pass the drawing

Ages: **6+** Numbers: **Any**

▶ A drawing version of the popular game of Chinese whispers.

Preparation: Pen and paper.

The first player draws something (it can be anything) on a piece of paper and shows it to the next player for 10 seconds. That person then has to draw what they saw, show it to the next player, and so on. The fun is in comparing the first with the final drawing. Make sure only the next person sees the picture.

Quick draw

Ages: **6+** Numbers: **Any, in teams**

▶ A drawing version of the popular board game of the same name.

Preparation: Cards with suggestions of what to draw, pens and paper.

The teams both send one player to the leader, who shows them a card with the object they must draw. They rush back and start sketching, with no words or gestures allowed. The first team to guess correctly wins the round. The game can be expanded to include verbs (such as running) and adjectives (like hot), or film titles.

Variations: 1 Each team lists eight films, books or TV shows for use by the opposing team. Each title should be written on a separate piece of paper and placed in a bowl, one bowl per team – do not get the bowls mixed up. These become the titles the opposing team has to try to draw, with teams taking it in turns to play. **2** Instead of drawing, the artist has to make plasticine or play-dough shapes to communicate the item.

The key in Quick draw is to be fast rather than accurate. It's amazing how a team can 'tune in' to each other's thinking.

Telegrams

Ages: **8+** Numbers: **Any, individually or in teams**

▶ A silly sentence-making game that has been popular for years.

Preparation: Pen and paper.

Each player calls out a letter until there are ten, which the players must write down in order. The challenge then is to create a telegram message where each word starts with one of the letters. Set a time limit of 10 minutes or less, after which players read out their messages. Award prizes for the cleverest or funniest telegram.

Variation: The telegram must refer to someone in the room.

Tell me what to draw

Ages: **6+** Numbers: **Any, in pairs**

▶ A talking and drawing game.

Preparation: Blindfolds, objects to draw, pen and paper.

Put the players into pairs sitting back to back, one blindfolded and equipped with pen and paper. Give the other player an object. They have to describe it without saying what it is, while their partner tries to draw what they hear. Swap roles. You'll need quite a few objects so that none are used twice.

Watch your back

Ages: **6+** Numbers: **Any**

▶ What does a drawing feel like?

Preparation: Sheet of paper pinned or taped to each player's back. Pencils.

Players stand in line and whoever is at the back draws a picture of an object on the paper of the person in front. Having only felt the drawing being done, that player then has to try to reproduce it on the back of the person in front, and so on up the line. Comparing the resulting pictures is bound to be interesting – and entertaining!

7 Racing games

Races are exciting: there's the sense of anticipation of the beginning, the alert watchfulness of the early stages, the rising sense of expectation as the finish line beckons, and the relief or disappointment of the result. Let's face it, adults get a bit carried away at times, and for some children, winning any kind of race (even the silliest race, and there are a few of those in this section) ensures the day will be memorable. Be prepared for rising temperatures and noise levels, and appoint an impartial judge to decide who has won.

Racing games

Only some of these races call for speedy legwork. Nimble fingers, quick minds and even a steady nose might be required instead. Make safety your top priority when setting up any running race, clearing away anything that could cause harm.

Baby race

Ages: **6**+ Numbers: **4**+

▶ A very silly racing game.

Preparation: Chairs, bibs and baby bonnet, plus baby feeding bottles.

Set out two chairs each with a bib and baby bonnet and a baby bottle half-filled with water. Divide the children into two teams and sit them down 10m (30ft) from the chairs. When you say 'Go', the first child in each team runs to a chair, puts on the hat and bib and drinks the water through the teat. First back to their team with the bib and hat removed wins. If you have plenty of bottles, you could set this up as a relay race.

Whatever their age, many children love pretending to be babies, and the Baby race gives them a fine excuse to do it.

Variations: 1 A helper puts the bib and hat on the child and holds the bottle for them. **2** Instead of a bottle of water, have a child feed their teammate some mushed-up food with a plastic spoon.

Bead relay

Ages: **6+** Numbers: **Any, in equal teams**
▶ A relay requiring nimble fingers.
Preparation: Set of beads, plus an egg carton for each team.

Agree a starting and turning point about 4m (12ft) away, and put a bowl of beads (or beans) at the turning point. Now place one egg carton for each team at halfway between these two points. The aim of the game is to put one bead in each cup of the egg carton, with players only able to pick up one bead at a time. First to fill their carton wins.

Variations: 1 Write a number between one and five under each cup. The team must put that number of beads in that cup. **2** Beads cannot be touched by hand, only with a spoon.

Bottle race

Ages: **6+** Numbers: **Even teams**
▶ A passing race using the knees.
Preparation: One plastic bottle per team.

Teams stand in a line and the aim of the game is to pass the bottle through the team, with the bottle only touching the knees. If the bottle is dropped, it must be picked up with the knees.

Cables

Ages: **8+** Numbers: **Pairs**
▶ An unusual ball-moving game.
Preparation: Equal lengths of string, ping pong balls or tennis balls for each pair.

Each pair has two lengths of string about 120cm (4ft) long. They hold them taut to create a track down which they must roll the ball. The first team to complete six rolls without dropping the ball wins.

Card sharks

Ages: **5+** Numbers: **Any, in equal teams**

▶ A hunting game through the house.

Preparation: Two packs of cards.

Before the party, hide all 52 of the cards around the house, arranging them so that they can be found without removing anything else. Now put players into teams and give each team a card from the second pack. Their task is to find its matching partner and bring it to you. Make a note of each team's success and give them another card until all are located. The top-scoring team wins.

Chin up!

Ages: **6+** Numbers: **Even teams**

▶ A passing race using the chin.

Preparation: One orange per team.

The team stands in line and the aim of the game is to pass the orange through the team (and back, if you wish). The orange must always be held under the chin. If it is dropped, the team has to start again.
Variation: This could be played as a circle game where the orange is passed around the circle and anyone who drops it is out. You'll need a referee for this one to decide who was in possession of the orange when it fell.

Chopstick race

Ages: **5+** Numbers: **Any**

▶ A test of manual dexterity.

Preparation: Sweets, bowls and chopsticks.

Give each player ten sweets, a bowl and a pair of chopsticks. They must get the sweets into the bowl using the chopsticks.

Variations: 1 Players must hold the chopsticks in one hand. **2** How many can they move in 1 minute?

Double packers

Ages: 7+ Numbers: **Any, in pairs**

▶ A tricky present-wrapping game.

Preparation: Parcel and wrapping paper for each pair.

Each pair must hold hands. Give each of them a parcel such as a shoe box or book, a sheet of wrapping paper or newspaper, sticky tape and a ribbon. They must wrap up the 'present' using their free hands. First pair wins, although you could also award a prize for the neatest wrapping.

Dress me!

Ages: 4+ Numbers: **Any**

▶ A team dressing-up game.

Preparation: Plenty of clothing for each team.

Put the children into teams, each with a set of clothing. The aim of the game is for them to dress one child in their team in as many items of clothing as possible in 2 minutes. The child being dressed is not allowed to put on anything themselves.

Egg and spoon race

Ages: 3+ Numbers: **Two equal teams**

▶ A classic sports' day event.

Preparation: Hard-boiled eggs, spoons.

This can be run as a simple race, or a relay for teams.

Variations: 1 Apple and spoon race. **2** Balloon and spoon race. **3** Use balls of cotton wool and have the team fill a bowl with them. **4** Run as a relay, but the egg or other object that is being carried must never be touched by hand.

Flap the kipper

Ages: **3**+ Numbers: **Any**

▶ A very old paper-propulsion game.

Preparation: Paper shapes, plus rolled-up newspapers.

This is best played on a hard floor. Cut out large kipper shapes from newspaper, and put one kipper in front of each child, who should also have a folded newspaper. They cannot touch the fish, but can flap their newspaper behind it to make it 'swim' across the surface to the finishing line.

Variations: 1 Try this as a relay race in teams. **2** Cut different shapes to match your party theme.

Children have been trying to master the technique of Flap the kipper for generations. The trick is to beat behind the paper shape because you need to make the air move.

Front and back

Ages: 7+ Numbers: **Equal teams**

▶ A 'pass it on' game that requires quick hands.

Preparation: Each team will need two buckets and plenty of objects to pass on.

Put plenty of objects to be passed on into one bucket for each team. See below for ideas. The team stands sideways in a line, facing the same way, with the full bucket at one end, the empty bucket next to it. The aim of the game is to pass all the objects through the team and into the second bucket. On its outward journey objects are passed to the front of each player, but on their return they must be passed behind the back of each player – so players have to keep switching from front to back. The winner is the first team to get the objects into the second bucket.

Here are some ideas for things to be passed on: wet soap, a peeled banana, an apple core, a slinky, a button or sequin, a beach ball or balloon.

Hot or cold?

Ages: 4+ Numbers: **Any**

▶ A traditional hunting game.

Preparation: Prizes hidden in the room or garden.

Hide a sweet in the room that the children must search for. You provide a running commentary of who is 'hot' (close) and who is 'cold' (way off) until the prize is found. Repeat.

Hunt the thimble

Ages: 3+ Numbers: **Any**

▶ A traditional party game that children love.

Preparation: Items to hide, such as lollipops or other sweets, other prizes, or even a thimble!

Either hide the object in advance or get players to wait in one room while you do so. Set some ground rules about which rooms they can search in and whether they'll need to lift or touch anything, then let the hunt begin.

Variation: Everyone has to stand in the room where the object is hidden. When they spot it, they sit down (some variants suggest that players say a phrase such as 'Huckle buckle beanstalk' at this point). Play stops when all are sitting, or after a few minutes, when the first person to find the objects says where they think it is. If they are right, they have won.

In a flap

Ages: **5+** Numbers: **Any**

▶ Slow and steady wins this race.

Preparation: Plastic plate and a feather for each competitor.

Agree the course and put all 'runners' on the start line. The aim of the game is to complete the race with the feather untouched on the plate. If it falls, it must be allowed to drop to the floor and the player must restart the race from the beginning.

It's very difficult to run when you're trying to keep something between your knees!

Knee-jerk relay

Ages: **6+** Numbers: **6+**

▶ A very silly racing game.

Preparation: Object for each team to carry.

Put the children into equal teams. Give the first player in each team an object such as a tennis ball or an orange. They must complete an agreed course with the object held between their knees, returning for the next player to do the same.

Variation: If one team is more skilful at the race, give them a smaller object, such as a matchbox or marble, to carry.

Marble derby

Ages: **6+** Numbers: **Any**

▶ A race requiring balance and patience.

Preparation: Each player needs a glass marble and two pencils.

The aim of this race is to complete the course (which should have bends in it) while balancing the marble on two pencils held in outstretched hands. If the marble falls or is touched by hand, you have to start again from the beginning.

Matchbox race

Ages: **5+** Numbers: **Equal teams**

▶ A classic nosey race.

Preparation: One matchbox sleeve per team.

The matchbox is passed through the team from nose to nose. If anyone touches it with their hand, the whole team has to start again.

The nerves and nose must be steady for the Matchbox race.

Minute race

Ages: **8+** Numbers: **Any**

▶ A quiet and calm walking game.

Preparation: You need something to time a minute exactly.

Ask everybody to remove their watches, and cover up any clocks that are in the room. Agree a route around the room that everybody must follow without stopping. The 'race' is to get to the finishing point in as close to a minute as possible.

Not knots!

Ages: **8+** Numbers: **Any, in even teams**

▶ A knot-tying and untying game with a twist.

Preparation: 1m (3ft) length of string for each team and a pair of gloves.

Teams stand in line and when the game starts the first player in each team ties a loose knot in the string and passes it on. Each player ties a knot and does the same, until the last in the line returns the string to the leader, who unties one knot and passes the string on for the next player to do the same. First team with a de-knotted length of string wins. This sounds easy until you are told that all players must be wearing gloves!

On your head

Ages: **8+** Numbers: **Even teams**

▶ A relay race with a difference.

Preparation: Inflated balloon/beach ball for each team.

Choose two or three teams of equal numbers. Agree a race course that players must walk with the balloon balanced on their head before handing the balloon to the next person in their team. If it drops, they have to let it land, then pick it up and replace it.

Variations: 1 Turn the course into an obstacle race.
2 The balloon must be held between the knees or batted in the air.

Orange putt

Ages: **7+** Numbers: **Any**

▶ A very silly fruit-moving race.

Preparation: Old tights and two oranges per player.

Two children each need the legs of an old pair of tights and two oranges. One fruit is placed down the tights, which are then tied round the waist. Swinging this as a 'bat', children then race to tap their other orange across a finishing line.

Variation: Try this with a broom and a ball.

Pairs

Ages: **7+** Numbers: **Any**

▶ A hunting-round-the-house game.

Preparation: Place various items around the house so they can be found without moving anything else.

Each hidden item should be part of a pair, such as a knife and fork, or pencil and eraser, while you keep its partner. Divide the players into teams and give each group one item, with instructions to complete the pair. If they succeed, make a note and give them another item. Highest scoring team wins.

Variation: A card version of this game is described as Card sharks on page 142.

Pass the balloon

Ages: **5+** Numbers: **Any, in equal teams**

▶ A balloon-passing game against the clock.

Preparation: Blown-up balloon for each team.

Each team sits in a circle. They must pass the

must know

Choosing teams

Lots of adults can recall the horrid feeling as children of being lined up to be chosen for teams with the inevitable result that one poor creature was left to be chosen last. Unpleasant at the best of times, it is completely inappropriate for a party. Here are some other ideas of how to choose teams:

▶ Number everybody from one to however many teams you want, then call all the 'ones' together as a team, then the 'twos' and so on until you have your teams.

▶ Hand out slips of paper with numbers or colours and call them out group by group.

▶ Just divide the group physically into half, then half again, to make four teams.

▶ Use colours or foods instead of numbers. Steer clear of football team names as they can create tension among young supporters.

Passsing a balloon behind your back can be tricky when it's wider than you! This activity can be adapted into a version of Pass the parcel, when whoever has the balloon when the music stops is out.

balloon to each other behind their backs as many times as they can within a set time – say, 1 minute (or the duration of a short song).

Pea relay

Ages: **6+** Numbers: **Even teams**

▶ A passing race using straws and peas.

Preparation: A straw for each player and a supply of frozen or dried peas.

This is a tricky team relay where players suck on the straw to keep the pea in place. The pea must be passed along the team from straw to straw, who must then re-start if it falls to the floor.

Variations: 1 Try using a tissue instead of a pea. **2** Turn the game into a race to transfer 20 peas from one cup to another.

Shoe hunt

Ages: **5+** Numbers: **Any**

▶ A frantic search that provides training for the first day back at school.

Preparation: None.

Everybody removes their shoes and puts them in one big pile, which should be mixed thoroughly. All players then go to the other end of the room, the lights are turned off (this is optional) and the aim of the game is to be the first person to get both shoes back on. Cue chaos!

Variations: 1 This can be played as a team game where shoes, coats and other clothing of your choice are piled up and the group works as a team to get everybody dressed upagain.
2 Draw around each guest's foot onto a piece of card or paper and cut out the shape. Jumble them all up and ask the guests to locate their 'foot'.

Shoebox race

Ages: **5+** Numbers: **Any**

▶ A very silly race.

Preparation: Ask each guest to bring two shoeboxes.

Tape the lids to the shoeboxes and cut a slit in the top. Each player slips their feet in (keep socks or tights and trousers on as the card may rub) and then run races with everyone wearing these big slippy 'shoes'.

Sponges

Ages: **5+** Numbers: **Any, in equal teams**

▶ A competition best held outdoors.

Preparation: Two buckets and a sponge for each team.

Each team stands in line with a water-filled bucket at one end and the empty bucket at the other. The aim of the game is to fill the empty bucket by passing and squeezing the wet sponge, so players need to be prepared to get rather soggy!

Stack race

Ages: **6+** Numbers: **Any, in equal teams**

▶ A passing and piling race.

Preparation: Set of ten clothes pegs or other objects for each team.

The team stands in line, at one end of which stands the pile of ten objects, such as clothes pegs, beanbags, toy bricks or stuffed animals. Each object is passed through the team, with no player being allowed to hold more than one at a time. The poor old player at the other end has to stack the objects in a tower so that only one touches the ground. If it topples, he must call out 'Timber' and the team cannot pass more items until the pile is rebuilt.

Step this way

Ages: **8+** Numbers: **Any number of pairs**

▶ A stepping stone race.

Preparation: Cut two big pairs of feet out of card for each team.

Teams must be split into pairs, and each of these must decide who is the footman, and who the stepper. Give each team two feet.

The Step this way game is an excellent exercise in coordination and cooperation: and it's fun, too!

The footman places the feet in front of the stepper, who must only walk on the card as he goes around the course. If a competitor's foot touches the ground, they have to start again.

Variations: 1 Put pairs into teams and make it a relay race. 2 Get players to put their own 'feet' in place. 3 Use sheets of newspaper instead of card.

String relay

Ages: **6+** Numbers: **Any, in equal teams**

▶ A race for speedy fingers and hands.

Preparation: Equal lengths of string for each team, plus an object with a hole for threading, like a ring, washer, or a mint or coin with a hole in it.

Teams thread on their object and tie the string to make a loop. Then each team stands in a circle with the loop held quite taut. The aim is to be first to pass the object round the team three times.

Variation: Try using a ring doughnut!

Tortoise race

Ages: **Any** Numbers: **Any**

▶ A race to be ... last!

Preparation: An agreed racing course.

In this race the aim is to be the last to finish. However, competitors are not allowed to stop moving at any time or to go sideways or backwards: they must keep going towards the line as slowly as possible. You will need a referee as alert as a hare.

Waiter slalom

Ages: **8+** Numbers: **Even teams**

▶ A race requiring a steady arm.

Preparation: Paper plate and a ping pong ball for each team.

Teams stand in lines with enough space for a player to run between them. This he must do while carrying the plate with the ball on it in the style of a waiter. He runs in and out, threading his way through the whole team and back before handing over the plate to the next player, whose place he then takes. The first team to complete the race wins.

8 Speaking games

This section includes several noise-making games that transform the room into a cacophonous zoo or a farmyard. Others are quieter but no less lively, calling for quick minds and tongues. Many speaking games have been played for a long time, but there are fun modern activities too. Included in this section are several useful ice-breaker games, and some where the tension can be almost unbearable: playing Botticelli (page 159) can be a truly nerve-wracking experience.

Speaking games

Try to choose speaking games that your guests will enjoy rather than endure: shy people will prefer team to individual activities, and for some folk, young and older, a game where they have to spell out loud is pure torture.

A what?

Ages: **8+** Numbers: **6+**

▶ A very old game that should be played at speed.

Preparation: Two simple objects to pass around like a ball and a cushion.

Everyone sits in a circle and one player passes an object to his neighbour and says 'This is a ...' and calls it anything he likes – a cat, banana, robot, or whatever. The recipient replies 'A what?' and the first player repeats what it is. The object is passed on with the same conversation happening each time, but simultaneously the first player passes another object the other direction, giving it an equally silly identification. The quick exchanges become very confusing when the objects pass each other.

Advertisements

Ages: **8+** Numbers: **Any**

▶ A good ice-breaking game requiring some preparation in advance.

Preparation: Cut out advertisements for products children like, such as chocolate bars, toys, etc.

When guests arrive, stick or pin one advertisement to their back. They have to ask the other people questions about it to guess what it is.

Variation: Use the wrappers themselves.

The alphabet game

Ages: **7+** Numbers: **6+**

▶ A quick-thinking game.

Preparation: Set of alphabet letter cards, set of category cards.

This is a word category game, so have some ideas ready to suit the players, such as sports, animals, foods or TV programmes and write each on a piece of paper or card. Shuffle the set of alphabet cards (you could omit Q, X and Z as they will be too tricky) and hold up one from each pile. The first player to call out a word that matches the category and starts with the target letter wins that letter card. So if 'sport' and 'P' are held up, they could say 'pole vault' and win the 'P' card. Category cards can be re-used, and the game ends when all the alphabet cards are given out. The player with most wins.

Animal bingo

Ages: **6+** Numbers: **Any**

▶ A noisy version of the popular game.

Preparation: Bingo cards, plus a way of generating numbers.

Play bingo as normal, with people crossing off numbers as they are called out. However, every time one of your numbers is called, you must make a loud animal noise (and that animal should not be repeated by anyone else). Instead of 'Bingo', the winner must sing 'How much is that doggy in the window?', 'Old MacDonald had a farm' or a similar animal song.

Animal snap

Ages: **5+** Numbers: **Any**

▶ A variation on the popular card game.

Preparation: A pack of playing cards.

Everyone demonstrates their animal noise, all of which must be different. Then you play 'Snap' in the normal way, but when a matching card appears, players must make the animal noise of the last person to put a card down. The first player to do this picks up the pack, and play continues until someone wins the whole pack.

Animal, vegetable or mineral

Ages: **8+** Numbers: **Any**

▶ A classic, very old quizzing game.

Preparation: None.

This game is also known as Twenty questions. A player secretly chooses an object, and then tells the other players only if it comes in the category of animal, vegetable or mineral. The categories can be defined as:

▶ Animal: any animal or anything made from animals (e.g. a leather shoe).

▶ Vegetable: anything that grows or comes from something that grows (e.g. trees, but also doors).

▶ Mineral: anything that is inorganic, such as glass or metal.

The other players can ask up to 20 questions, which must be answered either 'Yes' or 'No', before being allowed one guess of what the object is. If players are young, it is worth having a referee who knows what the object is and can help with answering tricky questions.

Backwards

Ages: **8+** Numbers: **Any**

▶ How good is your spelling?

Preparation: None.

One player spells a word backwards and the others race to say what the word is. Correct identifications score one point, but wrong guesses (and wrong spellings) lose a point.

Variation: Instead of spelling the word backwards, try saying it in reverse.

Blindfold race

Ages: **7+** Numbers: **Any, in equal teams**

▶ A lively race with instructions shouted by team members.

Preparation: Blindfolds, plus a racing circuit.

Divide the players into equal teams and set up a fairly small circuit. Remove any dangerous obstructions. One person from each team is blindfolded and they must get round the course while the rest of their team calls out instructions, after which the next player in each team puts on the blindfold and sets off. First team to finish wins.

Botticelli

Ages: **10+** Numbers: **4+**

▶ A game that really tests your biographical knowledge.

Preparation: None.

One brave volunteer thinks of a famous personality and states the initial letter of their name. For example if he has David Beckham in mind, he would say 'B'. The other players have to think of someone beginning with B (e.g. the composer Bach) and ask in this case 'Are you a famous composer?' If the player in the hot seat can think of a composer beginning with B, he can say 'No, I'm not Bach' (or any other such person with the right first letter) and the next player asks his question. However, if the volunteer cannot think of anyone who matches the question, the questioner states the answer he could have given and is then allowed to ask a direct question about the mystery personality, to which the volunteer can only answer 'Yes' or 'No'. This game can last quite some time (you could set a time limit of, say, 10 minutes per round) and is a real test of cultural knowledge.

You have to trust your partner in the Blindfold race.

Call my bluff

Ages: **10+** Numbers: **6+**

▶ A much-loved game used in a television programme of the same name.

did you know?

Call my bluff
Although it found fame as a television programme, this game began life as a Victorian parlour game called 'Dictionary' or 'Fictionary'.

Preparation: Supply each team with unusual words and definitions well in advance, or ask them to organize this themselves.

There are two teams of three players. In each round, the three members explain different definitions of the same (unusual) word. The opposing team has to decide which is the true definition, and which are the 'bluffs'. They take it in turns to do this and keep a score of correct answers. The game requires careful preparation, especially by the person who is to give the correct definition, as these can sometimes be rather scanty and players learn to recognize the reason for the lack of information (they couldn't make it up).

Can I come?

Ages: **8+** Numbers: **Any**

▶ A game where each player must work out the rule.

Preparation: Devise the rule for who can come.

This is really a trick game as players have to work out what the leader is doing. The leader starts by saying 'We're going on holiday. What are you going to bring?' Players take it in turns to suggest an object they will bring, finishing with the phrase 'Can I come?' The leader decides if they can come according to a rule based on its spelling or another characteristic. For example, the rule could be that you have to suggest something beginning with a letter in your name, or in the leader's name, or something that is yellow, or has wheels. You may need to offer little extra clues along the way.

Celebrity

Ages: **10+** Numbers: **Any**

▶ A quick-thinking game that changes with each round.

Preparation: Some suggestions of famous people to include.

All players write the names of five celebrities or characters on strips of paper, which are then folded and mixed in a bowl or bag. Divide everyone into two teams. The game now progresses in rounds in each of which players take turns to read a name and provide clues for the rest of their team. If you wish, you can score a point for each correct guess. When all the names have been used in a game you can return all the slips to the bowl and play again.

▶ Round one: Describe the person without naming them.
▶ Round two: Describe them in three words.
▶ Round three: Describe them in one word.
▶ Round four: Mime them.

Variation: Clues are given for the opposing team to guess the name.

Chinese whispers

Ages: **6+** Numbers: **10+**

▶ A traditional speaking and listening game.

Preparation: Write a few messages of at least ten words in advance. They can be silly or sensible.

Players sit in a circle or a line and you give one person a message card (make sure they can read it). They whisper it to

The enforced quiet of Chinese whispers can create a welcome oasis of calm during a hectic children's party.

the next person, and the message is sent round the group. You could play music in the background to prevent anyone overhearing it. The last person says the message out loud and it is compared with the original.

Coffeepot

Ages: **8+** Numbers: **Any**

▶ A traditional game of silly sentences and guessing.

Preparation: None.

While one player is out of the room the others agree a simple verb, such as 'walk' or 'eat'. When the other player returns, he asks questions where he substitutes the word 'coffeepot' for the verb, as in 'Do you coffeepot every day?' and 'Can a bird coffeepot?' Players must answer accurately 'Yes' or 'No'. If the word is guessed, whoever gave the last answer starts the next game. Set a time limit of about 3 minutes for each round.

Crambo

Ages: **8+** Numbers: **Any**

▶ A very old game of rhymes and guesses.

Preparation: None.

One player chooses a word and writes it down in secret. She then tells the group another word that rhymes with it. The aim is to discover the word by asking questions to which the answer rhymes with the secret word. So if told the secret word rhymes with 'dog', players might ask 'Are you a thick mist?' (fog) or 'Are you part of a clock?' (cog). If the first player cannot think of a rhyming answer or if the word is guessed, they lose the round. If people are stumped for, say, 5 minutes, the first player wins.

Definitions

Ages: **8+** Numbers: **Any**

▶ A game where you have to define a word.

Preparation: None.

This game can be played individually or in groups. Agree a letter that all words must start with for the round. The first player thinks of a three-letter word for it and makes up a definition. For example, if the letter is M, he could say 'M plus two letters is a diagram of the earth's surface', thinking of 'map'. The first player to identify the word has to think of a word of four letters beginning with M and define it, and so on until no one can think of a word to keep the round going. The game is then scored and a new initial letter chosen.

Earth, water, air and fire
Ages: **8+** Numbers: **Any**
▶ A quick-fire throwing, thinking and speaking game.
Preparation: A soft ball.

Children sit in a circle with a leader in the middle, who has the ball. They throw the ball to another child, saying either 'Earth', 'Water', 'Air' or 'Fire'. The child has to return the ball while saying an animal (Earth), fish (Water) or bird (Air), depending on which element the leader said. If the word is Fire, they have to run around pretending to put out the fire. Punish mistakes with forfeits (see page 47), and change the leader regularly.

Echoes
Ages: **7+** Numbers: **Any**
▶ A memory and sound guessing game.
Preparation: Blindfold.

One player is blindfolded. Five other players then make one sound each, either with their voices, or stamping, scraping or tapping. The blindfold is removed and that player has to re-create the sounds in the same order – so they have to identify how the noise was made, and recall what came before and after it. Have a leader making a brief note of each sound as it happens so that everyone can agree if the task was achieved.
Variation: Increase (or decrease in some cases) the number of sounds used.

Fizz buzz

Ages: **8+** Numbers: **Any**

▶ How well do you know your times tables?

Preparation: None.

This is a counting game where you have to concentrate very hard. Everyone sits in a circle and takes it in turns to count on one number ('1', '2', '3', etc.). However, if the number is in the five times table, such as 5 or 10, the player has to say 'Fizz'. Once players have mastered this idea, introduce the 'Buzz'. This is what must be said instead of multiples of seven, such as 14 and 21. For numbers that are in both the five and seven times tables (e.g. 35) the player has to say 'Fizz buzz'. A player making a mistake can be out, or asked to carry out a forfeit. Play until you are all exhausted but have a perfect grasp of your tables.

Variations: 1 Change the tables featured to, say, 3 and 4, or 6 and 8. **2** Say 'Fizz' for any number with a five in it (such as 51), 'Buzz' for numbers with a seven (e.g. 17), saying the word twice if the number is also a multiple (so 10 is now counted as normal because it has no five or seven but 15 is 'Fizz Fizz' because it is a multiple of five and has a five in it, and 75 is 'Buzz Fizz Fizz').

Food in the farmyard

Ages: **4+** Numbers: **Any, in teams**

▶ A noisy hunt for sweets.

Preparation: Sweets hidden around the house.

Hide the sweets and divide the group into teams. Each team must decide which animal they are and appoint a leader. All players except team leaders then set off on all fours to search the farmyard, as your home has become, for sweets. If they find any they must make the noise of their animal, which is the signal for the leader to come and collect the sweet. Only leaders can touch the sweets. The team that collects the most sweets wins.

Variation: Every player is a different animal, so the leaders must remember which animals are in their team.

Get it wrong

Ages: **5+** Numbers: **Any**

▶ A guessing game where the aim is not to be right.

Preparation: An egg cup filled with water.

Players sit in a circle. The leader writes a word on a piece of paper and conceals it before saying what type of word it is (e.g. 'colour'). Players then pass the egg cup round the circle, and as each receives it they say a word in that category. If they are wrong, the water is passed on; if they are correct, they have to pour the water on themselves.

Ghost

Ages: **8+** Numbers: **4+**

▶ A very popular game to test your vocabulary.

Preparation: None.

This is a word-building game where you lose if you complete the word. The first player says a letter, e.g. 'I'. If the second player says 'S' they would lose because they made 'is'. If they say 'G' (thinking of 'igloo') the game continues, only ending when a recognized word is spelt. Whoever completed it loses one life, and the game restarts. However, if players do not believe someone has a recognized word in their head, they can challenge the person to state the word that the letters help to form. Failure to name a word, or an incorrect challenge, loses a life. Decide the number of lives according to how many players you have.

Variations: 1 Try playing the game backwards! **2** Allow the addition of letters at the beginning and the end of the word – this can make the game last much longer.

---

must know

Helping shy speakers

Some children can be very shy about speaking in front of others, particularly to groups of people. Here are a few tips to help them:

▶ To talk with them, move them away from the prying eyes of the group and get down to their level (but not so close as to be scary).

▶ Don't apply pressure on them to speak to a group, it will make things worse.

▶ Find the person the child feels most comfortable with (it may be another child or an adult) and ask if they can speak out loud for them.

▶ Let them sit in on speaking games but make it clear they don't have to talk.

▶ Try to give them choices, like 'You can say your word to me or write it down on this paper' so that they don't feel as if they are on the spot.

▶ Set up a paired activity game (perhaps from the Pencil and Paper Games chapter) to help the child gain confidence.

Greetings your majesty

Ages: **4**+ Numbers: **10**+

▶ A game where players guess who is disguising their voice.

Preparation: None.

Choose someone to be king or queen, and stand them facing away from the group, or just blindfold them. Point to someone and ask them to say, 'Greetings your majesty' in a disguised voice. The royal person has to guess who said the phrase. Keep a tally and allow a few goes.

Variation: If you are having a birthday party, they could say, 'Happy birthday your majesty'.

Grocer's shop

Ages: **7**+ Numbers: **Any**

▶ An old word-guessing game with a food theme.

Preparation: None.

The first player says 'My father keeps a grocer's shop and he sells something beginning with...', finishing with the initial letter of the word. Other players have to guess the item, which must be something that could be sold by a grocer. The first one to get it right starts the next round.

Ha! ha! ha!

Ages: **6**+ Numbers: **4**+

▶ The aim of this game is to keep a straight face.

Preparation: None.

Players sit or stand in a circle. One says 'Hee!' to his neighbour, who then turns to his neighbour and says 'Hee, hee!' Everybody has to keep a straight face while a 'Hee!' is added each time. Anyone who smiles, laughs or says the wrong number of 'Hee's is out, and can then go anywhere and pull faces at the other players, but not make any sounds. Eventually you will have a straight-faced winner.

Variations: 1 Allow the 'out' players to make noises too. **2** Change 'Hee' to other phrases, perhaps related to a party theme.

Children are quite accustomed to sitting in circles for activities such as speaking games. This arrangement keeps everyone involved.

Hesitation

Ages: **8+** Numbers: **Any, in equal teams**

▶ Can you talk without saying 'um'?

Preparation: Cards or slips of paper with words written on or pictures of objects.

This is a game designed to expose how often people use verbal 'ticks'. One player at a time is given a card and has to speak about the object making reasonable sense for 30 seconds. Pauses of more than 3 seconds, use of hesitation or indecision-disguising words such as 'er', 'um' or 'like' lose the team a point each time. Completing the 30-second speaking task earns five points.

I packed my bag ...

Ages: **6+** Numbers: **4+**

▶ A test of your memory.

Preparation: None.

Players sit in a circle. The first says 'I packed my bag and in it I put ...' and names something beginning with the letter A.

The next player must repeat this phrase and the item and add something beginning with B, and so the game continues. Players who make mistakes, such as omitting items or putting them in the wrong order, are out. It might be worth setting a time limit rather than allowing the list to grow too long.
Variation: Players add one number each time (e.g. 'one apple, two bins, three calculators ...')

Last letter
Ages: **9+** Numbers: **Any**
▶ A quick-thinking, fast-talking word game.
Preparation: None.

Everyone sits in a circle and all agree a broad category, such as nature or sports. The first person says any word that could be in that category, such as 'flower'. The next player has to say a word that matches the category beginning with the last letter of the previous word, in this case 'r', so they could say 'rain'. Give each player up to 10 seconds to find a word or they are out.

Make a word
Ages: **8+** Numbers: **Any**
▶ Who can make a word first?
Preparation: None.

In this game players add one letter at a time in a bid to be the first to make a recognized word. Others can challenge if they do not believe the letter another player has added would eventually make a word. Players can add a letter to a recognized word if they can show that they are helping to make a longer word (for example if three players combine to create 'WAS' the next could add 'H' to make 'WASH', and the next could add 'B', thinking of 'WASHBOARD'. They will be motivated to do this because whoever cannot add a letter loses a point. This game is a good introduction to the skills needed for Ghost on page 165.

Menagerie

Ages: **6+** Numbers: **Any**

▶ How good is your memory?

Preparation: A collection of about ten cuddly toys and some name cards.

Show players the menagerie of animals and explain each has their own name. You could just say them, or it might be fairer to put a name card by each one. Make the names similar (e.g. Rob, Robbie, Robert, Roberto, Ronald, Raul). Then remove the name cards and if you are feeling particularly mean, play a different game to distract everybody, before bringing the animals back in and giving points to the first player to call out a correct name. Restrict players to three guesses – don't let them call out the whole list each time. Whoever remembered the most names wins.

Now was that bear called Rob or Robbie?

Menu

Ages: **6+** Numbers: **4+**

▶ A food-suggestions game.

Preparation: None.

One player is appointed chef. He says 'I'm planning the menu for tonight but I'm only cooking food with a ... in it', stating a letter (which cannot include Q, X, Y or Z). Players take it in turns to suggest foods that could be on the menu, all containing the stipulated letter (it doesn't have to be at the beginning). Anyone who can't think of one is out until there is just one winning player left.

Mindreader

Ages: **8+** Numbers: **Any**

▶ Can you justify what you just said?

Preparation: None.

The leader thinks of a word and, for fairness, writes it down. Then he says 'Read my mind.' Everyone takes turns to guess what he is thinking of. They are very unlikely to be correct, so then he shows or tells his word. Now each player has the chance to justify their word by arguing that it is linked with the one written down. For example, if they guessed 'bucket' and the word was 'window', they could claim you use a bucket to clean the window, so the words are linked.

Mr and Mrs

Ages: **18+** Numbers: **Pairs**

▶ A game for couples, which formed a long-running TV series.

Preparation: Have questions ready to be asked.

One half of the couple leaves the room and must not hear the proceedings as their partner is asked a series of questions about their life together, likes and dislikes, habits and routines. The answers are noted then the process is repeated with the roles swapped and the two sets of answers compared, which is often very entertaining.

My little bird

Ages: **6+** Numbers: **Any**

▶ A traditional speaking and actions game.

Preparation: None.

Everyone stands in a circle. One player says, 'My little bird is lively, lively', then names something, followed by the word 'fly' (so he could say, '... dogs fly.') If the thing named can fly, players flap their arms. If it cannot, they stay still. Anyone making a mistake is out and the winner is the last one left.

Variations: 1 Change the 'fly' element to 'swim' or 'run' or

other active verbs. **2** Ask the players to fly in the style of the flying object, e.g. ' ... fairies fly', '... aeroplanes fly'.

Keep the pace fast for My little bird to cause maximum confusion and hilarity.

Name six

Ages: **8+** Numbers: **Any**

▶ A lively word game.

Preparation: A soft ball or other object that can be passed around.

Everyone sits in a circle apart from the leader who is outside or in the middle. The ball is passed round the circle until the leader calls 'Stop', followed by a letter of the alphabet. Whoever is holding the ball passes it on but has to call out six things starting with that letter before the ball comes round full circle to them again. If she can't, she swaps with the leader.

Variation: The things named must be linked by a set theme, such as a party theme, sports, or anything else that is suitable.

Social skills

Speaking and listening games help children to develop social skills and are particularly useful at the start of a party as they make people talk to each other, break the ice and help everyone have a more enjoyable time as a group. Speaking and listening skills are important in all areas of life, so by playing these games you are helping the children's development.

No yes

Ages: **3**+ Numbers: **Any**

▶ A very old copying game.

Preparation: None.

One person comes to the front and the others ask them questions. They are not allowed to say 'Yes' or 'No', but must answer in some way within 5 seconds. Anyone uttering the forbidden words is out immediately. Allow up to ten questions.

Noah's ark

Ages: **6**+ Numbers: **Any, in pairs**

▶ A noisy 'find your partner' game.

Preparation: A set of paired animal cards.

Give everyone a card with an animal drawn or written on it, ensuring that you issue two of each. When you say 'go' each person makes their animal noise and seeks out their partner.

Variations: 1 Try this game in the dark, with at least one of the pair blindfolded. **2** Play in groups of three, with one of the group being the baby.

One at a time

Ages: **6**+ Numbers: **Any**

▶ A tricky guessing game.

Preparation: Have some suggested words or categories ready. Pen and paper.

A player announces a category (such as beasts, or sports, or anything else fairly general) and writes down a word that matches it. He then announces the first letter, and the other players guess what the word is. Two wrong guesses mean he states the second letter, and so one, until the word is identified. The player scores one point for every letter he had to state. Writing the word down prevents cheating by changing it.

One octopus

Ages: **6**+ Numbers: **Any**

▶ A listing and memory testing game.

Preparation: None.

Players sit in a circle. The first says 'One octopus'. The next must repeat this and add 'two...' finding something that beings with the letter 't' (because it is the first letter of 'two'). The third person lists these two items adding a third, also starting with 't' (or 'th' if you want to use sounds rather than letters). Anyone making mistakes is out, until there is one (probably rather weary-tongued) player left.

Over here!

Ages: **6**+ Numbers: **Any**

▶ A noisy game best played away from the neighbours.

Preparation: Blindfold, animal cards or slips for each player.

Everyone stands in a large circle apart from one blindfolded person, who stands in the middle and is told to, 'Find the dog'. Each player checks their animal card and makes the noise of that animal while the blindfolded seeker tries to move towards the barking sound.

Variation: The blindfolded person is told to go to a person in the room – but everyone tries to sound like them.

Password

Ages: **8**+ Numbers: **Any, in teams**

▶ A word definition game.

Preparation: Cards or slips of paper with words on.

A player from the first team takes one of the slips. The aim of the game is for your team to guess the word without you saying it. The player gives a one-word clue that must not include, or be a variant of, the target word (e.g., if the target word was 'surfboard', hints such as 'surfing' or 'board' would

8 Speaking games

not be allowed, but 'waves' or 'riding' would be fine). If their team identifies the word, they score ten points. If not, the paper is given to one player from the opposing team (who heard the first clue and the guess) and another one-word clue offered. Success now earns nine points. Play continues with the score for success descending by one each time until the word is identified or ten goes have passed.

Poor kitty

Ages: **6+** Numbers: **Any**

▶ A favourite from the days of the parlour game.

Preparation: Blindfold.

Everyone stands in a circle except for one blindfolded player in the middle. Players can move slowly around the circle while the blindfolded person walks forward and touches someone. That person has to say 'Poor kitty' and meow like a cat, and the listener has to guess their identity. If he succeeds, they swap places.

Relationships

Ages: **8+** Numbers: **Any**

▶ A game of word association.

Preparation: None.

Players sit in a circle and someone starts the game by saying a word. The person next to them must say a word related to it (e.g. 'football' could follow 'pitch' or 'goal'). So the game continues until someone can't think of a word and hesitates too long. Players can challenge at any time if they think the words cannot be related. A failed challenge or turn puts that player out, until there is no one left in the game (or you can just set a time limit).

Scary sounds

Ages: 5+ Numbers: **Any**

▶ A chance to spook out your guests.

Preparation: Slips of paper with scary sounds written on them.

The scary sounds could include a creaking door, rattling chains, ghostly moan, approaching thunder, footsteps on the stairs. With the lights down low, each player takes a turn at reading a slip (a torch will be spookily handy) and making their sound with any part of their body. Others have to guess the sound.

Seat of truth

Ages: **6+** Numbers: **Any, in two teams**

▶ A listening and running game.

Preparation: Two chairs, plus prepare some statements ready for the game.

Place the two chairs at opposite ends of the room, and it is agreed which is the seat of truth, and which is the seat of falsehood. Both teams are positioned in the middle of the room, but only one player from each team plays in each round. The leader reads out a statement, which should be worded so that it is hard to tell immediately whether or not it is true. The players must decide if it is true or false and run to sit in the appropriate chair – first to get there wins the point if they are right.

Simon says

Ages: 3+ Numbers: **Any**

▶ A very old copying game.

Preparation: None.

One person is the leader. They say 'Simon says' and add an action such as 'put your hands on your

did you know?

Port and starboard
A naval version of Simon says, in which the captain of the ship instructs his crew, is called Port and starboard, and all the actions are related to running a ship. The key phrase is 'Captain says'.

The game of Simon says should be played at an increasing pace to add to the excitement.

head'. Everybody has to copy, unless the leader gives an instruction that doesn't start with 'Simon says', in which case no one should do it. Players are out if they disobey these rules – it helps to have a referee.

Variation: Players do not get 'out', but must stand out for a count of 20.

Smelly sausages

Ages: 5+ Numbers: **Any**

▶ A game where you try to keep a straight face.

Preparation: None.

One player comes to the front. The others ask them questions and they must always answer 'Smelly sausages', however little sense it makes. The person answering is out if they laugh. Allow up to ten questions.

Variation: Change the phrase to anything else that will sound ridiculous as an answer.

Squeak, piggy, squeak

Ages: **6+** Numbers: **Any**

▶ A classic voice recognition game.

Preparation: Blindfold, plus a cushion.

Blindfold one player, turn them round a few times, then tell them to find someone else in the room, put the cushion on their lap and sit on it. The blindfolded player must then say 'Squeak, piggy, squeak' and whoever they are sitting on must squeal like a pig. If the blindfolded player recognizes their voice, they say the name and if they are right, they change places. Otherwise, play continues.

Piggies have been squeaking in disguise since at least Victorian times, when the game was very popular.

Taboo

Ages: **10+** Numbers: **Any**

▶ A game that requires excellent spelling and vocabulary.

Preparation: None.

Taboo means 'forbidden' and in this game one letter is 'taboo' and no word that contains it can be used. The leader selects this letter and starts asking the others any question of his choosing. They must answer accurately (one word answers are fine) but cannot use the taboo letter. Anyone doing so is eliminated until you have a winner.

Three things

Ages: **8+** Numbers: **Any**

▶ A game to build the vocabulary.

Preparation: A ball.

Players sit in a circle and whoever has the ball rolls it to another while calling out an occupation such as 'doctor', 'teacher' or 'dustman'. The person receiving the ball must quickly name three things associated with that job. They then roll the ball to someone else. Slow answers are punished with a forfeit.

Variation: The objects must all contain a certain letter.

Tongue twisters

Ages: **6**+ Numbers: **Any**

▶ These have manifested much merriment for millennia (that's a tongue twister!).

Preparation: Have some suggestions ready (see below).

This can be played as a game if you count how many times someone can say the phrase in, say, 30 seconds, or it can just be a fun activity. Here are some suggested tongue twisters:

▶ She saw shy sheep.

▶ She sells sea shells on the seashore, she sells sea shells no more.

▶ Red lorry yellow lorry.

▶ A big bug bit the little beetle but the little beetle bit the big bug back.

▶ Minnie Mouse makes many marshmallows for Mickey Mouse to munch on.

▶ Betty bought butter but the butter was bitter, so Betty bought better butter to make the bitter butter better.

▶ Moses supposes his toeses are roses but Moses supposes erroneously for Moses he knowses his toeses aren't roses like Moses supposes his toeses to be.

▶ A fly and a flea in a flue were caught so what did they do? Said the fly, 'Let us flee!' Said the flea, 'Let us fly!' So they flew through a flaw in the flue.

▶ A Tudor who tooted a flute tried to tutor two tooters to toot. Said the two to their tutor 'Is it harder to toot or to tutor two tooters to toot?'

21

Ages: **8**+ Numbers: **Any**

▶ A tricky counting game involving strategy.

Preparation: None.

Players sit in a circle, neighbours taking it in turns to count consecutively up to 21. The aim is to avoid saying the final number. Each player may count on the next one or two numbers, but if they say two numbers (e.g. '12, 13') the direction of play is reversed. Any mistakes are punished with a forfeit, as is whoever ends up (reluctantly) saying '21'.

20-second list

Ages: **8+** Numbers: **Any**

▶ A game for quick-witted fast talkers.

Preparation: Have some ideas for categories, such as 'colours' or 'sports'.

Players take it in turns to name as many things as they can in the category in 20 seconds. Obviously the category should be changed each time. Keep a tally so you can have a winner if you wish.

Two minutes of fame

Ages: **10+** Numbers: **Any, in pairs**

▶ A celebrity-spotting game.

Preparation: Blank slips of paper and pens.

All players write the names of four famous people or things, such as film or book titles, each on a separate slip of paper, which is folded and put in a bowl. In each pair there will be a clue giver and a guesser. The giver reads a slip and describes the famous person or thing without naming them, starting a new one every time their partner guesses correctly. A tally is kept for 2 minutes, when it is the turn of the next pair.

What animal?

Ages: **7+** Numbers: **Any**

▶ An identity guessing game.

Preparation: None.

One person leaves the room and the others decide on a creature that they have to guess. When they come in, they ask questions like 'Can I swim?' and 'Do I have a nest?' The rest of the group can only answer yes or no. The child has to guess what animal they are.

Variations: 1 Play this game as an ice-breaker at the start of the party by sticking pictures or labels of animals on guests' backs. They have to ask the other people in the room questions about their animal, and again, the answers can only be yes or no. **2** Instead of animals, you could choose objects linked with a party theme.

What did we say?

Ages: **10+** Numbers: **Any, in teams**

▶ Can you work out what phrase is being called?

Preparation: List of suggested phrases.

Agree a category for a set of phrases, like film titles, proverbs, TV programmes or song titles. One team leaves the room and agrees their phrase (e.g. *The Sound of Music*) and who is going to call out which word. If there are more players than words in the phrase, players can double up and share a word. On their return they all shout out their one word simultaneously and the other team or teams have to guess what the phrase is. If they succeed, they swap roles, if not, the first team tries again.

What did we say is a lively and noisy game particularly suitable for playing across the generations because you can choose a theme suitable for the ages of different players.

What's my line?

Ages: **8+** Numbers: **Any**

▶ A variation on a famous early TV quiz.

Preparation: A standby list of occupations.

One person goes out of the room, and the others choose an occupation that they will have to guess, for example teacher. When she returns, she asks everyone in the group for something she must buy to do her job, and tries to guess the occupation from their answers. If she can't, in the next round she asks what she would wear. The game ends when she identifies the job. You need to make sure everyone understands what the job is before the questioning part of the game.

Variation: Players have to guess which celebrity they are.

Word tennis

Ages: **8+** Numbers: **Pairs or teams**

▶ A game demanding quick thinking.

Preparation: None.

Choose a category for words, such as sports, foods or your party theme. The pairs or teams now take turns to say a word that fits the category, with the 'rally' ending when a player is stuck for a word.

Variation: If the rounds are lasting too long, set a rule that the words have to include a certain letter, or (harder) start with it, or are a set number of letters long.

Zoo queue

Ages: **4+** Numbers: **Any**

▶ A memory game that works best in groups of 6–10.

Preparation: None.

Players sit in a circle. The first says 'One cat' (it doesn't matter what the animal is), the next adds to this by saying 'One cat, two rabbits'. The game continues with players reciting all the numbers of animals, adding to the list each time. If they forget one, they are out, and the game continues.

What games do you need?

Quiet games

Suitable for very young children

Team games

want to know more?

Websites

www.bbc.co.uk/dna/h2g2/C798
www.child-tea-party-game-ideas.com/tea-party-games.html
www.comeparty.co.nz
www.ezinearticles.com/?Kid-Birthday-Party-Games—-Under-10s&id=73677
www.funandgames.org
www.gameslinks.com/Party_Games/
www.holidaycook.com/party-games
www.kids-partycabin.com
www.partygamecentral.com
www.party-games.zaural.ru/party-games
www.thefunplace.com

Books

The Biggest Book of Party Games Ever, Kerrin Edwards (Carlton)
The Children's Party Book: For Birthdays and Other Occasions, Anne Thomas (Floris Books)
Family Party Games: 100 Fun Games for All Occasions, Peter Arnold (Hamlyn)
501 Party Games for Kids, Penny Warner (Hinkler Books)
Great Big Book of Children's Games, Debra Wise (McGraw-Hill)
Kid's Party Games and Activities, Penny Warner (Prentice Hall)
Oranges and Lemons: Musical Party Games for Young Children, Karen King (Oxford University Press)
Practical Parenting Party Games, Jane Kemp and Clare Walters (Hamlyn)
'Practical Parenting' Party Games: Over 90 Games to Make Your Children's Party Go with a Swing!,
    Jane Kemp, Clare Walters (Hamlyn)

Index

Index

Acknowledgments

Lyra Publications wish to thanks all the models for their patience
and enthusiasm: Adrianne, Amy, Anthea, Ashley, Corrie, Emily,
Esther, Felicity, Freddie, Georgia, Hattie, Holly, Isobel, Josh, Katie,
Keith, Matthew, Maxim, Morgan, Naomi, Nicola, Oliver, Patrick,
Peter, Phoebe, Rosi, Sofia and Thea. It was fun.

⟐ **Collins** need to know?

**Look out for these recent titles in Collins' practical and accessible
need to know? series.**

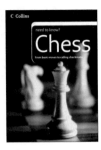

Other titles in the series:

**To order any of these
titles, please telephone
0870 787 1732 quoting
reference 263H.
For further information
about all Collins books,
visit our website:
www.collins.co.uk**